New York City Travel Guide with 3-Day, 5-Day, 7-Day itineraries

Welcome to the Ultimate **Manhattan Travel Guide**, your go-to resource for exploring the vibrant and bustling heart of New York City! This guide is designed to help you make the most of your time in Manhattan by providing detailed information on attractions, accommodations, dining, transportation, and more. Whether you're visiting for business or leisure, our curated itineraries will ensure you experience the best that Manhattan has to offer.

In this guide, you'll find a comprehensive breakdown of the city's most iconic sights, hidden gems, and local favorites. We've organized the information into a series of carefully planned itineraries that cater to different interests and timeframes. Each itinerary covers a full day in Manhattan, highlighting key attractions, restaurants, and activities that suit a variety of tastes and budgets.

In addition to our itineraries, the guide includes valuable information on the cost of living in Manhattan, providing you with a clear understanding of the expenses you may encounter during your trip. From accommodations and dining to transportation and attractions, we've got you covered with budget-friendly tips and recommendations.

Get ready to explore the dynamic city of Manhattan and immerse yourself in its diverse culture, awe-inspiring architecture, and world-class entertainment. Let this Ultimate Manhattan Travel Guide be your trusted companion as you embark on an unforgettable adventure through the heart of New York City.

Contents

New York City Travel Guide with 3-Day, 5-Day, 7-Day itineraries 1

1. Introduction 9
    1.1 A Brief History of New York City 9
    1.2 Getting to Know Manhattan 12
    1.3 Navigating the City: Public Transportation and Beyond 14

2. Iconic Sights and Attractions 21
    2.1 Timeless Classics: Empire State Building, Statue of Liberty, and Central Park 21
    2.2 Museums and Galleries: From The Met to MoMA 26
    2.3 Architectural Marvels: The Flatiron Building, Woolworth Building, and Oculus 30

3. Hidden Gems: Off-the-Beaten-Path Adventures 33
    3.1 Unusual Museums: The Tenement Museum, The City Reliquary, and The Museum of the Moving Image 33
    3.2 Quirky Neighborhoods: DUMBO, Red Hook, and the High Line 37
    3.3 Secret Gardens: Elevated Acre, 6BC Botanical Garden, and the Lotus Garden 38

4. Culinary Delights: Diverse Flavors of NYC 40
    4.1 Exploring Manhattan's Food Halls: Chelsea Market, Hudson Yards, and Gansevoort Market 40
    4.2 Ethnic Enclaves: Little Italy, Chinatown, and Koreatown 42
    4.3 Sustainable Dining: Farm-to-Table Restaurants and Greenmarkets 43

5. Arts and Culture Scene 45
    5.1 Broadway and Beyond: Theater, Musicals, and Off-Broadway 45
    5.2 Live Music Venues: Jazz, Indie Rock, and Classical 54
    5.3 Film Festivals and Independent Cinemas 56

6. Sports and Recreation 60
    6.1 Major Sports Teams: Yankees, Mets, Knicks, and Rangers 60
    6.2 Alternative Sports Activities: Indoor Rock Climbing, Paddleboarding, and Biking 62
    6.3 Parks and Green Spaces: Prospect Park, Battery Park, and Riverside Park 64

7. Shopping in Manhattan 67
    7.1 Luxury Boutiques: Fifth Avenue, Madison Avenue, and SoHo 67
    7.2 Unique Local Shops and Independent Designers 68
    7.3 Vintage and Thrift Stores: The Ultimate Guide 70

8. Nightlife and Entertainment 74

- 8.1 Rooftop Bars with Stunning Views..74
- 8.2 Speakeasies and Hidden Bars: Prohibition-Era Glamour 77
- 8.3 Comedy Clubs and Cabaret Shows 80
- 8.4 Explore New York City by Night 83

9. Family-Friendly Activities 91
- 9.1 Kid-Friendly Museums and Interactive Exhibits...91
- 9.2 Urban Adventures: Zoos, Aquariums, and Amusement Parks....................92
- 9.3 Educational and Fun Workshops for the Whole Family..............................94

10. Seasonal Events and Festivals 97
- 10.1 Winter Wonderland: Ice Skating, Holiday Markets, and Festive Lights 97
- 10.2 Spring Blossoms: Cherry Blossoms, Macy's Flower Show, and Easter Parade........98
- 10.3 Summer in the City: Outdoor Movies, Concerts, and Street Fairs 100
- 10.4 Fall Foliage: Halloween Celebrations and Thanksgiving Traditions 101

11. Practical Information...104
- 11.1 Accommodation: Hotels, Hostels, and Vacation Rentals.........................104
- 11.2 Where to Stay in NYC: Exploring Manhattan's Vibrant Districts...................105
- 11.2 Staying Connected: Wi-Fi, Cell Phones, and Internet Cafes....................109
- 11.3 Health and Safety: Travel Insurance, Hospitals, and Emergency Contacts.......110
- 11.4 Best Tips and Recommendations for your travel to NYC 112
- 11.5 Best Budget-Friendly Dining Options in Manhattan 120
- 11.6 NYC Passes To Purchase Before You Go to NYC 122
- 11.7 How Expensive is Manhattan 124
- 11.8 Bucket List..127

12. Customized Itineraries 129
- 12.1 3-Day, 5-Day, and 7-Day Itineraries 129
  - 12.1.1 3-Day Itinerary...129
  - 12.1.2 5-Day Itinerary...133
  - 12.1.3 7-Day Itinerary...136
- Online Maps with all the Locations of the 7-Day Travel Itinerary 139

Our Detailed 3-Day Travel Itinerary to NYC and Manhattan............................141

Day 1 in NYC: Arrival 141
- 10:00 Arrival in New York City at LaGuardia Or JFK International. 141

- 10:30 Transportation from the Airport to the Hotel 141
- 11:30 Arrive and check into your hotel. 141
- 12:00 Grab a bite to eat at Pound & Pence 55 Liberty St. 141
- 13:00 Visit the Statue of Liberty 142
- 15:10 Explore the Famous Times Square 143
- 19:00 Dinner at The Jekyll & Hyde Club 145
- 21:00 Attend a performance at the Upright Citizens Brigade, a renowned comedy club in the nation. 145
- 23:00 Return to the hotel and unwind 146

Lower Manhattan 1st Day Map 147

Zooming on: Transportation 148

Zooming on: Public Transportation Directions Day 1 151

Day 2 in NYC: Shopping, Famous Restaurants & More 152
- 09:00 Breakfast in Herald Square at Tick Tock Dinner 481 8th avenue and shopping at Macy's 152
- 12:00 Enjoy a Sandwich at Tick Tock Diner 152
- 11:00 Take a ride IN the Empire State Building 152
- 13:00 Grays Papaya, Lincoln Center, and The Central Park Zoo 154
- 15:30 Lunch at Serendipity 3, 225 East 60th street 156
- 17:00 See the city at night 157
- 19:00 Dinner at the first pizzeria in the United States, Lombardi's Pizza, 32 Spring Street 158
- 20:30 Take a stroll around Little Italy 159
- 21:30 Have a little fun at Greenwich Village Country Club, 110 University Place 159
- 12:00 AM Return to Hotel 160

2nd Day Map in NYC 161

Zooming on: Day 2 Directions 162

Day 3: Intrepid Museum, Grand Central 164
- 09:00 Breakfast at Amy's Bread, 672 9th Avenue 164
- 10:30 Visit the Intrepid Sea, Air & Space 164
- 12:00 City Cruise Experience 166
- 15:00 Have a late lunch at Shake Shack, 691 8th Avenue 168
- 16:00 Head back to the hotel to check out 169
- 18:00 Shopping in the Woodbury Commons Outlet Mall 169

Day 3 NYC Map 171

- Zooming on: Day 3 Directions 172
- The Craziest Experience You Can Have in NYC 173
- Day Trips from New York City 174
  - Washington D.C. Day Trip from New York City (around 140 USD per person) 174
  - Explore the Rich Historical Heritage of Philadelphia 175
  - Enjoy a Day in the Middle of Nature at Bear Mountain State Park 175
  - Have Some Fun at the Six Flags Great Adventure in New Jersey 176
  - Unwind on a Charming Beach: Fire Island 176
- Thank You 178
- Copyright Notice 180

1. Introduction
1.1 A Brief History of New York City

New York City, the largest metropolis in the United States, has a rich and storied history that spans over 400 years. From its humble beginnings as a Dutch trading post to its present-day status as a global financial and cultural capital, New York has undergone a remarkable transformation.

The Early Days: Native Americans and Dutch Settlement

Before European settlers arrived, the area now known as New York City was inhabited by the Lenape people, a Native American tribe who lived in the region for thousands of years. In 1524, Giovanni da Verrazzano, an Italian explorer sailing for France, became the first European to enter New York Harbor. However, it wasn't until 1609 that the English explorer Henry Hudson, commissioned by the Dutch East India Company, ventured up the river that would later bear his name.

In 1624, the Dutch West India Company established a trading post on the southern tip of present-day Manhattan, which they called New Amsterdam. The Dutch settlers traded with the local Native Americans, primarily for beaver pelts, which were highly valued in Europe. The Dutch also purchased the island of Manhattan from the Lenape in 1626 for a small collection of trade goods, in a transaction that has become a symbol of the city's founding.

English Rule and the Birth of New York

The Dutch rule of New Amsterdam ended in 1664 when the British captured the colony during the Second Anglo-Dutch War. The English renamed the settlement New York, in honor of the Duke of York, who later became King James II of England. Under British rule, New York City grew rapidly, becoming an important port and commercial center.

The American Revolution and the Early Republic

New York City played a significant role in the American Revolution, serving as a battleground, a center of political activity, and the nation's first capital.

The city was occupied by British forces from 1776 to 1783, and many New Yorkers were divided in their loyalties between the Crown and the revolutionaries. In 1783, the last British troops left New York City, marking the end of the Revolutionary War.

In 1785, New York City became the capital of the newly formed United States, and George Washington was inaugurated as the country's first president at Federal Hall on Wall Street in 1789. The city's role as the capital was short-lived, however, as the government moved to Philadelphia in 1790.

The 19th Century: Growth and Immigration

Throughout the 19th century, New York City experienced significant growth and change. The opening of the Erie Canal in 1825 connected the city to the Great Lakes region, further solidifying its status as a major commercial hub. Advances in transportation, such as the introduction of the steamboat and the construction of the city's first railroads, fueled the city's expansion.

The 19th century also saw a massive influx of immigrants, as millions of people from Europe, Asia, and the Americas arrived in search of a better life. New York City became a melting pot of cultures, with neighborhoods like Little Italy, Chinatown, and the Lower East Side serving as home to diverse communities.

During this period, the city's landscape was also transformed by the construction of iconic structures such as the Brooklyn Bridge and Central Park, as well as the development of the city's first skyscrapers.

The 20th Century: Transformation and Turmoil

In the early 20th century, New York City emerged as a global leader in finance, media, and the arts. The city's population continued to grow, and by the 1920s, it had become the world's largest city, with more than 10 million residents. The city's cultural scene flourished during the Jazz Age, with Harlem becoming the epicenter of the Harlem Renaissance, a period of immense artistic and intellectual achievement among African Americans.

However, the city was not immune to the hardships of the 20th century. The Great Depression hit New York City hard, with unemployment rates skyrocketing and thousands of people becoming homeless. The city rebounded during World War II, as it played a crucial role in the war effort, serving as a major port for shipping and a hub for the manufacture of war supplies.

Post-war New York saw an explosion of growth and development. The city's iconic skyline was reshaped with the construction of monumental structures like the United Nations Headquarters, the Empire State Building, and the World Trade Center. The city also solidified its position as a global center for art, fashion, and entertainment, with the rise of abstract expressionism, the birth of the New York School of poets, and the establishment of Broadway as the heart of the American theater.

The latter half of the 20th century brought challenges for New York City, including economic decline, rising crime rates, and social unrest. The city faced bankruptcy in the 1970s, but it managed to recover in the 1980s and 1990s due to fiscal reforms, revitalized industries, and a sharp decrease in crime.

The tragic events of September 11, 2001, marked a turning point for New York City. The terrorist attacks on the World Trade Center shocked the world and deeply affected the city's residents. In the aftermath, New Yorkers demonstrated resilience and unity, rebuilding the World Trade Center site with the new One World Trade Center and the National September 11 Memorial and Museum.

21st Century New York City: A Modern Metropolis

Today, New York City stands as a testament to its remarkable history, a thriving metropolis that is continually evolving and reinventing itself. As a global center of finance, media, technology, and culture, the city attracts millions of tourists and new residents each year, drawn to its iconic landmarks, diverse neighborhoods, and vibrant arts scene.

The city continues to grapple with challenges such as income inequality, affordable housing, and climate change, but it remains a beacon of hope and opportunity for people from all walks of life.

In conclusion, the history of New York City is one of growth, transformation, and resilience. From its beginnings as a Dutch trading post to its current status as a global capital, the city has faced numerous challenges and emerged stronger each time. The spirit of New York City is one of ambition, creativity, and perseverance, and its rich history serves as a foundation for the continued growth and innovation that lie ahead.

1.2 Getting to Know Manhattan

Manhattan, the heart and soul of New York City, is a bustling island that captures the imagination of millions around the world. Home to iconic landmarks, historic neighborhoods, and a vibrant culture, Manhattan offers an unforgettable experience for visitors and residents alike. To fully appreciate this remarkable borough, it's important to get acquainted with its geography, neighborhoods, and unique characteristics.

Geography and Orientation

Manhattan is located at the center of the five boroughs that make up New York City. Surrounded by the Hudson River to the west, the East River to the east, and the Harlem River to the north, Manhattan covers an area of approximately 23 square miles. It is roughly 13 miles long and 2 miles wide at its widest point.

The island is divided into three main sections: Lower, Midtown, and Upper Manhattan. Lower Manhattan is home to the Financial District, including Wall Street and the New York Stock Exchange, as well as Battery Park and the 9/11 Memorial. Midtown Manhattan is where you'll find iconic attractions like Times Square, the Empire State Building, and the Museum of Modern Art. Upper Manhattan is further divided into the Upper East Side, Upper West Side, and Harlem, each with its own distinct character and attractions.

Neighborhoods

Manhattan is made up of a diverse range of neighborhoods, each with its own unique charm and personality. Some of the most famous neighborhoods include:

1. Greenwich Village: Known for its bohemian atmosphere, historic brownstones, and vibrant arts scene, this neighborhood is also the birthplace of the modern LGBTQ+ rights movement.
2. SoHo: Renowned for its cast-iron architecture, high-end boutiques, and art galleries, SoHo is a shopper's paradise.
3. Chelsea: Home to the High Line, Chelsea Market, and a thriving LGBTQ+ community, Chelsea is also famous for its contemporary art galleries.
4. Tribeca: A hub of chic lofts, celebrity residents, and the annual Tribeca Film Festival, this neighborhood is one of Manhattan's most upscale areas.
5. Chinatown: A bustling enclave rich in culture and history, Chinatown offers authentic cuisine, shops, and vibrant street life.
6. Harlem: A cultural powerhouse, Harlem is known for its rich African-American history, the Apollo Theater, and the soulful sounds of jazz.

Getting Around

Manhattan's grid system, which dates back to the early 19th century, makes it relatively easy to navigate. Streets run east to west, while avenues run north to south. The grid system begins at 1st Street in the south and goes up to 220th Street in the north. Fifth Avenue divides the island into east and west sections, with street numbers increasing as you move away from Fifth Avenue.

Public transportation is the most convenient and cost-effective way to explore Manhattan. The Metropolitan Transportation Authority (MTA) operates the city's extensive subway and bus network, which covers all five boroughs. The subway system, in particular, is an efficient way to travel within Manhattan, with numerous lines and frequent service.

Taxis, rideshare services, and Citi Bike (the city's bike-sharing program) are also popular options for getting around the city. Walking is another great way to experience Manhattan's unique neighborhoods and attractions, as many sights are within close proximity to one another.

In conclusion, getting to know Manhattan is essential for anyone planning a visit to New York City. With its iconic landmarks, diverse neighborhoods, and efficient public transportation, Manhattan offers a wealth of experiences that cater to every interest and taste. By familiarizing yourself with the geography and neighborhoods of the island, you'll be well-prepared to make the most of your time in this unforgettable city.

1.3 Navigating the City: Public Transportation and Beyond

New York City is renowned for its extensive and efficient public transportation system, which makes navigating the city a breeze for both visitors and residents. In addition to its world-famous subway system, the city also boasts a vast network of buses, commuter trains, ferries, and even bicycles for rent. In this section, we'll provide an overview of the various modes of transportation available in New York City, as well as some tips for making the most of your time in the Big Apple.

Subway

The New York City subway system, operated by the Metropolitan Transportation Authority (MTA), is the largest and busiest in the United States. With 472 stations and 27 lines, the subway is the backbone of the city's public transportation network, providing service 24 hours a day, seven days a week. Trains are frequent, and most stations are accessible via MetroCard, a rechargeable fare card that can be purchased at station vending machines.

When navigating the subway, pay attention to the line colors, numbers, or letters, as well as the direction of travel (Uptown or Downtown). Express trains, which skip certain stations, are marked with a white circle around the line number or letter, while local trains, which stop at all stations, have a black circle. Subway maps are available online, at station booths, and in subway cars.

Navigating the New York City Subway system can be a breeze with the right information at hand. Here's some super practical information to help you get around with ease during your visit:

Subway Fares:

- Single Ride Ticket: $3.00
- Pay-Per-Ride MetroCard: Minimum $5.50; you can add value to the card as needed
- Unlimited 7-Day MetroCard: $33.00
- Unlimited 30-Day MetroCard: $127.00

Note: Reduced fares are available for seniors and disabled passengers.

Purchasing MetroCards: You can buy MetroCards from vending machines or staffed booths at subway stations. Vending machines accept cash, credit, or debit cards, while booths take cash only. You can also purchase cards at select convenience stores and newsstands.

Subway Maps: To find a subway map, visit the Metropolitan Transportation Authority (MTA) website at https://new.mta.info/maps or use their interactive map at https://map.mta.info/. Additionally, you can pick up a printed map at any staffed subway booth or use navigation apps like Google Maps or Citymapper on your smartphone.

Buses

The MTA also operates an extensive bus network throughout the five boroughs, with more than 300 routes and 16,000 stops. Buses are particularly useful for reaching destinations not served by the subway, as well as for traveling within neighborhoods. Bus stops are typically located on street corners and are marked with a blue and white sign displaying the route number and destination. MetroCard is accepted on buses, as well as exact change in coins.

Riding the bus in New York City can be a great way to see the city and reach your destinations. Here's some super practical information to help you navigate the bus system with ease during your visit:

Bus Fares:

- Standard fare (using a MetroCard or OMNY): $2.75 per ride
- Single Ride Ticket: $3.00 (available for purchase at vending machines in subway stations)
- Unlimited 7-Day MetroCard: $33.00
- Unlimited 30-Day MetroCard: $127.00

Note: Reduced fares are available for seniors and disabled passengers.

Purchasing MetroCards: You can buy MetroCards from vending machines or staffed booths at subway stations. Vending machines accept cash, credit, or debit cards, while booths take cash only. You can also purchase cards at select convenience stores and newsstands.

Bus Maps and Schedules: To find bus maps and schedules, visit the Metropolitan Transportation Authority (MTA) website at https://new.mta.info/maps or use their interactive map at https://map.mta.info/. You can also use navigation apps like Google Maps or Citymapper on your smartphone for real-time bus information.

Tips for Riding NYC Buses:

1. Know your bus route and stop: Familiarize yourself with the bus route and stop locations before boarding to ensure a smooth journey.

2. Have your MetroCard or exact change ready: Prepare your MetroCard or exact change ($2.75 in coins, no pennies or bills) before boarding the bus to avoid delays.
3. Board at the front and exit at the rear: Enter the bus through the front door and exit through the rear door to keep the flow of passengers moving efficiently.
4. Request your stop: If your stop is not a major one, press the yellow or gray "stop request" strip near the windows or pull the stop request cord above the windows to signal the driver.
5. Be mindful of bus etiquette: Offer your seat to those in need, avoid eating or drinking on the bus, and keep your belongings secure.

Commuter Trains

For those looking to explore beyond the city limits, New York City offers several commuter rail services. The Long Island Rail Road (LIRR) connects Manhattan with Long Island, while Metro-North Railroad serves the northern suburbs and parts of Connecticut. New Jersey Transit provides train service between Manhattan and destinations in New Jersey. These trains typically depart from major stations such as Penn Station or Grand Central Terminal, and fares vary depending on the distance traveled.

Commuter trains in New York City are a convenient way to travel between the city and its suburbs, as well as to nearby cities in the tri-state area. Here's some super practical information to help you navigate the commuter train system with ease during your visit:

Commuter Train Systems:

1. Long Island Rail Road (LIRR): Serving Long Island with connections to Manhattan, Brooklyn, and Queens.

2. Metro-North Railroad: Connecting Manhattan with Westchester, Putnam, and Dutchess counties in New York, as well as Fairfield and New Haven counties in Connecticut.
3. New Jersey Transit (NJT): Serving New Jersey with connections to Manhattan and Philadelphia.

Fares: Fares vary depending on the specific train line, the distance traveled, and the time of day. For detailed fare information, visit the respective train system's website:

- LIRR: https://new.mta.info/lirr
- Metro-North: https://new.mta.info/mnr
- NJT: https://www.njtransit.com/

Purchasing Tickets: You can purchase tickets at station ticket offices, vending machines, or through each train system's respective mobile app. It's best to buy tickets before boarding, as onboard purchases may incur a higher fare.

Train Maps and Schedules: To find train maps and schedules, visit the websites of the specific train systems:

- LIRR: https://new.mta.info/maps
- Metro-North: https://new.mta.info/maps
- NJT: https://www.njtransit.com/train-to

You can also use navigation apps like Google Maps or Citymapper on your smartphone for real-time train information and directions.

Ferries

New York City's extensive waterways offer a unique and scenic mode of transportation. The Staten Island Ferry is a free service that connects Manhattan to Staten Island, offering stunning views of the Statue of Liberty and the Lower Manhattan skyline. Other ferry services, such as NYC Ferry and New York Water Taxi, provide connections between Manhattan, Brooklyn, Queens, and the Bronx, with fares generally ranging from $2.75 to $7.00 per ride.

Citi Bike

Citi Bike is New York City's bike-sharing program, offering a fun and environmentally friendly way to explore the city. With thousands of bikes available at docking stations throughout Manhattan, Brooklyn, Queens, and the Bronx, Citi Bike is a convenient option for short trips and sightseeing. Users can purchase a single ride, a day pass, or a monthly membership, and bikes can be returned to any docking station in the system.

Taxis and Rideshare Services

Yellow cabs are an iconic symbol of New York City and can be hailed on the street or picked up at taxi stands. Fares are metered, and taxis accept both cash and credit card payments. Rideshare services like Uber and Lyft are also widely available throughout the city and can be accessed using smartphone apps.

In conclusion, navigating New York City is made easy thanks to its diverse and efficient public transportation options. From the subway to ferries, there is a mode of transportation to suit every preference and itinerary.

Taxi fares in New York City can vary depending on factors such as traffic, time of day, and distance. However, here are some typical prices for taxi rides between popular places in NYC:

1. JFK Airport to Manhattan: $52 flat fare (plus tolls and a $4.50 surcharge during peak hours)
2. LaGuardia Airport to Midtown Manhattan: Approximately $35 - $45 (including tolls)
3. Penn Station to Times Square: Approximately $10 - $15

4. Times Square to Central Park: Approximately $10 - $15
5. Greenwich Village to Upper East Side: Approximately $20 - $25
6. Financial District to Midtown Manhattan: Approximately $20 - $30

Please note that these prices are rough estimates and may vary. There is an initial charge of $2.50, and the meter adds $0.50 for every 1/5 mile or 60 seconds in slow traffic. There's also a $0.50 night surcharge between 8 PM and 6 AM, and a $1 peak-hour surcharge from 4 PM to 8 PM on weekdays.

In addition to taxis, consider using rideshare apps like Uber or Lyft for convenient and potentially more cost-effective transportation options in NYC. Always remember to factor in waiting time, traffic, and surge pricing when estimating the cost of your trip.

2. Iconic Sights and Attractions

2.1 Timeless Classics: Empire State Building, Statue of Liberty, and Central Park

New York City is home to an array of world-famous landmarks and attractions that have stood the test of time. Among these timeless classics, three icons stand out as must-see destinations for any visitor to the city: the Empire State Building, the Statue of Liberty, and Central Park. These iconic sites not only showcase the city's history and architectural prowess but also offer unforgettable experiences that capture the essence of New York.

Empire State Building

Located in Midtown Manhattan, the Empire State Building is an Art Deco masterpiece that has graced the city's skyline since its completion in 1931. Standing at 1,454 feet (including its broadcast antenna), this skyscraper was the tallest building in the world until 1970 and remains a symbol of New York City's architectural ingenuity.

Visitors can ascend to the building's two observation decks on the 86th and 102nd floors, which offer breathtaking panoramic views of the city. The 86th floor observatory features an open-air deck, while the 102nd floor offers an enclosed viewing area with floor-to-ceiling windows. Tickets can be purchased in advance online or at the building's ticket office.

Empire State Building Address: 350 5th Ave, New York, NY 10118

Visiting Hours: Daily from 8 AM to 2 AM (last admission at 1:15 AM)

Website: https://www.esbnyc.com/

Tickets: You can purchase tickets online through the official website or on-site at the Empire State Building ticket office.

Ticket Options:

1. Standard Entry: Includes access to the 86th-floor observatory. Prices are $42 for adults, $36 for children (6-12), and $40 for seniors (62+).

2. Express Pass: Includes expedited entry and access to the 86th-floor observatory. Prices are $78 for adults, $72 for children (6-12), and $76 for seniors (62+).

Booking: We recommend booking your tickets online in advance to save time and avoid long lines. You can book tickets through the official website: https://www.esbnyc.com/buy-tickets

Hours to Visit: The best times to visit the Empire State Building are early in the morning (8 AM - 11 AM) or late at night (after 10 PM) to avoid crowds. Peak entrance times are between 11 AM and 2 PM, as well as one hour before and one hour after sunset.

Tips:

- All guests must pass through security to access the observatory.
- There is a 102nd-floor observatory with an additional fee. You can upgrade your ticket at the observatory ticket office (on the 2nd floor) or at the 86th-floor kiosk.
- High-power binoculars are available on the observatory deck for a minimal cost, not included in the ticket price.
- Dress warmly, as it can be chilly on the 86th-floor observatory deck.
- Street sales agents outside of the building are not employed by the Empire State Building Observatory and are not authorized to sell Express upgrades.

Additional Information: The Empire State Building offers a variety of attractions, including an interactive exhibit on the 80th floor and a sustainability exhibit on the 2nd floor. The building is wheelchair accessible, and multilingual audio guides are available for rent.

Statue of Liberty

A gift from France to the United States in 1886, the Statue of Liberty is a symbol of freedom and democracy that has welcomed millions of immigrants to America's shores. Standing on Liberty Island in New York Harbor, this colossal neoclassical sculpture was designed by Frédéric Auguste Bartholdi and dedicated by President Grover Cleveland.

To visit the Statue of Liberty, visitors must take a ferry from Battery Park in Lower Manhattan or Liberty State Park in New Jersey. The ferry ticket includes access to Liberty Island and Ellis Island, where the Ellis Island National Museum of Immigration offers a fascinating glimpse into the history of immigration in the United States. Visitors can also reserve tickets to enter the statue's pedestal or climb to the crown, though these tickets are limited and often sell out well in advance.

Statue of Liberty Address: Liberty Island, New York, NY 10004

Visiting Hours: Daily from 8:30 AM to 4 PM (last ferry from Battery Park departs at 3:30 PM)

Website: https://www.nps.gov/stli/index.htm

Tickets: Tickets can be purchased online through the official ferry provider, Statue Cruises, or on-site at the ticket office in Battery Park (New York) or Liberty State Park (New Jersey).

Ticket Options:

1. Reserve Ticket: Includes ferry transportation and access to Liberty Island and Ellis Island. Prices are $23.50 for adults, $12 for children (4-12), and $18 for seniors (62+).

2. Pedestal Reserve Ticket: Includes ferry transportation, access to Liberty Island and Ellis Island, and entry to the pedestal of the Statue of Liberty. Prices are $23.50 for adults, $12 for children (4-12), and $18 for seniors (62+).

3. Crown Reserve Ticket: Includes ferry transportation, access to Liberty Island and Ellis Island, and entry to the crown of the Statue of Liberty. Prices are $28.50 for adults, $17 for children (4-12), and $23 for seniors (62+).

Booking: We recommend booking your tickets online in advance to secure your preferred time and date, as crown tickets sell out quickly. You can book tickets through the official ferry provider, Statue Cruises: https://www.statuecruises.com

Hours to Visit: The best times to visit the Statue of Liberty are early in the morning (first ferry departs at 8:30 AM) or later in the afternoon to avoid crowds. The site tends to be busiest between 11 AM and 2 PM.

Tips:

- All guests must pass through security to board the ferry and access Liberty Island.
- Crown access requires climbing a narrow, 377-step spiral staircase, and large bags or backpacks are not allowed.
- Comfortable shoes and weather-appropriate clothing are recommended for the visit.
- Audio tours are available in multiple languages and are included with your ticket.

Additional Information: The Statue of Liberty is a national monument managed by the National Park Service. It is located on Liberty Island, which is accessible only by ferry. The ferry ticket also includes access to Ellis Island and its Immigration Museum. The site is wheelchair accessible, with some limitations for crown access.

Central Park

Designed by landscape architects Frederick Law Olmsted and Calvert Vaux, Central Park is a sprawling urban oasis in the heart of Manhattan. Covering 843 acres, this public park features lush green spaces, picturesque lakes, and winding paths that offer a welcome respite from the city's hustle and bustle.

Central Park is home to a variety of attractions, including **the Central Park Zoo**, the **Loeb Boathouse**, the **Bethesda Terrace**, and the iconic **Bow Bridge**. Visitors can also enjoy outdoor activities such as rowboating, biking, or simply strolling along the park's many walking trails. Throughout the year, the park hosts numerous events, including concerts, outdoor theater performances, and ice-skating during the winter months.

The Empire State Building, Statue of Liberty, and Central Park are timeless classics that showcase the rich history and enduring appeal of New York City. These iconic attractions offer unforgettable experiences and should be at the top of every traveler's itinerary when visiting the Big Apple. Whether marveling at the cityscape from high above, celebrating freedom and democracy, or finding tranquility amidst nature, these timeless destinations capture the spirit of New York City in all its diversity and splendor.

Central Park Address: Central Park, New York, NY 10024 (The park extends from 59th Street to 110th Street, and from Fifth Avenue to Central Park West)

Visiting Hours: Open daily from 6 AM to 1 AM

Website: https://www.centralparknyc.org/

Tickets: Entry to Central Park is free, but certain attractions within the park may require tickets or fees.

Popular Attractions:

1. Central Park Zoo: Open daily from 10 AM to 5 PM (5:30 PM on weekends). Tickets range from $12 to $18 per person.

2. Conservatory Garden: Open daily from 8 AM to dusk. Admission is free.
3. Rowboat rentals at Loeb Boathouse: Open seasonally from 10 AM to 5:30 PM. Rentals cost $20 per hour (cash only) with a $20 cash deposit.
4. Guided Tours: The Central Park Conservancy offers a variety of guided tours. Prices and schedules can be found on their website: https://www.centralparknyc.org/tours

Getting There: Central Park is easily accessible by subway, bus, taxi, or on foot. The closest subway lines are the A, B, C, D, 1, 2, 3, N, Q, R, and W trains.

Tips:

- Central Park is large and can take hours to explore on foot. Consider renting a bicycle or using a Citi Bike to cover more ground.
- There are several playgrounds, picnic areas, and scenic spots throughout the park, so be sure to bring snacks, water, and a blanket or towel to sit on.
- The park has several restrooms and food vendors, but it's recommended to bring your own water bottle and snacks.
- Download the official Central Park app (available for iOS and Android) for an interactive map, self-guided tours, and up-to-date information on events and attractions.

2.2 Museums and Galleries: From The Met to MoMA

New York City is a global center for art and culture, boasting an impressive collection of museums and galleries that cater to a wide range of interests. Two of the city's most renowned institutions, The Metropolitan Museum of Art (The Met) and The Museum of Modern Art (MoMA), offer visitors a chance to immerse themselves in the world of art, from ancient masterpieces to contemporary works. These iconic institutions are essential stops for art enthusiasts and casual visitors alike.

The Metropolitan Museum of Art (The Met)

Located along the eastern edge of Central Park, The Metropolitan Museum of Art, commonly referred to as The Met, is one of the largest and most prestigious art museums in the world. Established in 1870, The Met's vast collection spans more than 5,000 years of human history and encompasses over two million works of art.

The museum's galleries showcase a diverse range of art and artifacts, including European paintings, Egyptian temples, Greek and Roman sculptures, and Medieval armor. Highlights of the museum's collection include works by renowned artists such as Vincent van Gogh, Rembrandt, and Leonardo da Vinci, as well as the ancient Egyptian Temple of Dendur.

The Met also operates two additional locations: The Met Cloisters, which focuses on European medieval art and architecture, and The Met Breuer, dedicated to modern and contemporary art. A single admission ticket grants access to all three locations within a three-day period.

The Metropolitan Museum of Art (The Met) Address: 1000 Fifth Avenue, New York, NY 10028

Visiting Hours: Open Sunday to Tuesday and Thursday from 10 AM to 5 PM, and Friday to Saturday from 10 AM to 9 PM. The Met is closed on Wednesdays.

Website: https://www.metmuseum.org/

Tickets: General admission is $25 for adults, $17 for seniors (65 and over), and $12 for students. Children under 12 enter free with an adult. The ticket includes same-day admission to The Met Cloisters and The Met Breuer.

Where to Book: You can purchase tickets online on The Met's website, at the museum ticket counters, or through third-party platforms like CityPASS or New York Pass. Booking online may offer skip-the-line privileges.

Getting There: The nearest subway lines are the 4, 5, and 6 trains, stopping at the 86th Street station. The M1, M2, M3, and M4 buses also stop near the museum.

Tips:

- The Met offers free guided tours of the museum, which are included with your admission ticket. Check the museum's website for tour schedules.
- The museum is large, so consider setting aside at least 3-4 hours to explore the vast collection.
- Audio guides are available for an additional fee ($7 for adults, $6 for seniors, $5 for students, and free for children under 12). They are offered in several languages.
- The museum has several dining options, including cafés and a more formal restaurant. However, prices can be high, so you may want to consider eating elsewhere before or after your visit.
- The Met Store offers a wide range of souvenirs, including art prints, books, and unique gifts.

The Museum of Modern Art (MoMA)

Founded in 1929, The Museum of Modern Art, or MoMA, is a world-renowned institution dedicated to showcasing and preserving modern and contemporary art. Located in Midtown Manhattan, MoMA's collection features over 200,000 works of art, including painting, sculpture, photography, film, design, and more.

MoMA's galleries are home to some of the most iconic works of the modern era, including Vincent van Gogh's "The Starry Night," Salvador Dalí's "The Persistence of Memory," and Pablo Picasso's "Les Demoiselles d'Avignon." The museum also hosts temporary exhibitions, film screenings, and educational programs, providing a dynamic and engaging experience for visitors.

In addition to its main location, MoMA operates MoMA PS1, a contemporary art center located in Long Island City, Queens. This affiliate institution focuses on experimental and cutting-edge works by emerging artists and hosts the popular Warm Up summer music series.

The Museum of Modern Art (MoMA) Address: 11 West 53rd Street, New York, NY 10019

Visiting Hours: Open daily from 10:30 AM to 5:30 PM, and until 8:00 PM on Fridays. MoMA is closed on Thanksgiving Day and Christmas Day.

Website: https://www.moma.org/

Tickets: General admission is $25 for adults, $18 for seniors (65 and over), and $14 for students. Children 16 and under enter free with an adult. Admission is free for all visitors on Fridays from 5:30 PM to 8:00 PM.

Where to Book: You can purchase tickets online on MoMA's website, at the museum ticket counters, or through third-party platforms like CityPASS or New York Pass. Booking online may offer skip-the-line privileges.

Getting There: The nearest subway lines are the B, D, F, and M trains, stopping at the 47-50 Streets - Rockefeller Center station. The E and M trains stop at the 5th Avenue/53rd Street station. Several buses, such as the M1, M2, M3, M4, M5, and M7, also stop near the museum.

Tips:

- MoMA offers free daily guided tours of the museum, which are included with your admission ticket. Check the museum's website for tour schedules.

- The museum is large, so consider setting aside at least 2-3 hours to explore the extensive collection.

- Audio guides are available for an additional fee ($5 for adults, $4 for seniors, $3 for students, and free for children under 16). They are offered in several languages.

- MoMA has multiple dining options, including cafés and a more formal restaurant. However, prices can be high, so you may want to consider eating elsewhere before or after your visit.

- The MoMA Design Store offers a wide range of souvenirs, including art prints, books, and unique gifts inspired by the museum's collection.

2.3 Architectural Marvels: The Flatiron Building, Woolworth Building, and Oculus

New York City's skyline is a testament to its architectural prowess, with a diverse array of structures that showcase various styles and historical periods. Among the city's many architectural marvels, the Flatiron Building, Woolworth Building, and Oculus stand out as exceptional examples of design and engineering. These iconic structures not only contribute to the city's distinctive skyline but also serve as a window into the evolution of architectural styles throughout New York City's history.

Flatiron Building

Completed in 1902, the Flatiron Building is a striking example of Beaux-Arts architecture and one of New York City's earliest skyscrapers. Designed by architect Daniel Burnham, the building is instantly recognizable by its unique triangular shape, which was inspired by its location at the intersection of Fifth Avenue, Broadway, and 23rd Street. At 22 stories and 307 feet tall, the Flatiron Building was once one of the tallest structures in the city.

The building's distinctive shape and elegant facade, clad in limestone and terracotta, have made it an enduring symbol of New York City and a popular subject for photographers and artists. While the Flatiron Building currently houses offices and is not open to the public, its exterior can be admired from the surrounding streets or from the vantage point of Madison Square Park.

Woolworth Building

The Woolworth Building, completed in 1913, is a stunning example of neo-Gothic architecture and was once the tallest building in the world at 792 feet. Designed by architect Cass Gilbert, the building was commissioned by Frank W. Woolworth, the founder of the Woolworth retail chain, as a testament to his business empire.

The building's intricate terra-cotta facade is adorned with ornamental details, including gargoyles and a series of panels depicting the story of the building's construction. The spectacular lobby features vaulted ceilings, marble floors, and a stained-glass ceiling, showcasing the opulence and grandeur of the early 20th-century architectural style. While the Woolworth Building now primarily serves as a residential and office space, guided tours of the lobby are available for those interested in exploring its architectural splendor.

Oculus

The Oculus, completed in 2016, is a modern architectural marvel designed by renowned Spanish architect Santiago Calatrava. This striking structure serves as the World Trade Center Transportation Hub, connecting multiple subway lines and the PATH train to New Jersey. The Oculus's design features a soaring, ribbed structure that resembles the wings of a dove in flight, symbolizing hope and rebirth following the tragic events of September 11, 2001.

In addition to its transportation function, the Oculus houses a vast shopping center and dining options within its airy, light-filled interior. The building's unique design and symbolic significance make it a must-visit destination for architecture enthusiasts and visitors to the World Trade Center complex.

3. Hidden Gems: Off-the-Beaten-Path Adventures

3.1 Unusual Museums: The Tenement Museum, The City Reliquary, and The Museum of the Moving Image

New York City's diverse cultural landscape is home to an array of unique and unusual museums that offer visitors a chance to explore lesser-known aspects of the city's history and artistic heritage. Among these off-the-beaten-path institutions, The Tenement Museum, The City Reliquary, and The Museum of the Moving Image stand out as fascinating destinations that provide an alternative perspective on New York City's rich cultural tapestry.

The Tenement Museum

Located on Manhattan's Lower East Side, The Tenement Museum offers a glimpse into the lives of immigrant families who called New York City home in the 19th and early 20th centuries. Housed in a restored tenement building at 97 Orchard Street, the museum offers guided tours that showcase the building's restored apartments, which have been furnished to reflect the living conditions of various immigrant families who resided there.

Through its immersive exhibits, The Tenement Museum brings to life the stories of immigrants from different backgrounds and their pursuit of the American Dream. In addition to its apartment tours, the museum offers walking tours of the Lower East Side neighborhood and hosts various events and programs that explore themes related to immigration, diversity, and social history.

The Tenement Museum Address: 103 Orchard Street, New York, NY 10002

Visiting Hours: Open daily from 10:00 AM to 6:30 PM, except on major holidays. The museum is closed on Thanksgiving Day, Christmas Day, and New Year's Day.

Website: https://www.tenement.org/

Tickets: Admission to the Tenement Museum is through guided tours only. Ticket prices for tours range from $25 to $35 for adults, $20 to $30 for seniors (65 and over), and $15 to $25 for students and children (6-17 years old). Children under 6 are not permitted on most tours.

Where to Book: You can purchase tickets online on the Tenement Museum's website, by phone at (877) 975-3786, or in person at the museum's Visitor Center. Advance booking is recommended, as tours often sell out.

Getting There: The nearest subway lines are the F train, stopping at the Delancey Street/Essex Street station, and the J, M, and Z trains, stopping at the Essex Street station. The B39 bus also stops near the museum.

Tips:

- The Tenement Museum offers various tours, including building tours that explore the history and lives of immigrant families who lived in the tenement buildings, and neighborhood walking tours that provide a broader context of the Lower East Side's history.
- Tours last approximately 1 hour and have limited capacity. Be sure to arrive at least 15 minutes before your scheduled tour time.
- Photography is not allowed inside the museum's historic tenement buildings, but you can take photos outside and in the Visitor Center.
- The museum is not wheelchair accessible due to the historic nature of the tenement buildings, so it may not be suitable for visitors with limited mobility.
- There is no café or dining area at the museum, but the Lower East Side has many dining options within walking distance.

The City Reliquary

Nestled in the heart of Williamsburg, Brooklyn, The City Reliquary is a small, community-focused museum dedicated to celebrating the unique and often overlooked history of New York City. Founded by a group of local enthusiasts, the museum features a quirky collection of artifacts and ephemera that showcase the city's past, from vintage subway tokens and fragments of famous landmarks to historical maps and photographs.

The City Reliquary's rotating exhibitions and community events focus on local history, urban archaeology, and the city's diverse neighborhoods. This hidden gem of a museum offers visitors a chance to delve into the lesser-known aspects of New York City's past and connect with the vibrant community that makes the city so special.

The City Reliquary Address: 370 Metropolitan Ave, Brooklyn, NY 11211

Visiting Hours: Open Thursday through Sunday from 12:00 PM to 6:00 PM.

Website: https://www.cityreliquary.org/

Tickets: Admission to the City Reliquary is $7 for adults, $5 for seniors (65 and over) and students. Children under 12 are admitted for free.

Where to Book: Tickets can be purchased in person at the museum's entrance. Advance booking is not necessary.

Getting There: The nearest subway station is the Metropolitan Avenue station on the G and L lines. The B24, B48, and Q54 buses also stop near the museum.

Tips:

- The City Reliquary is a small museum, so you can expect to spend about an hour exploring its exhibits.
- Photography is allowed inside the museum, but flash photography may be restricted for certain exhibits.

- There is no café or dining area at the museum, but the surrounding Williamsburg neighborhood has a wide variety of dining options within walking distance.

The Museum of the Moving Image

Situated in Astoria, Queens, The Museum of the Moving Image is dedicated to the art, history, and technology of film, television, and digital media. Housed in a former film studio, the museum features interactive exhibits that allow visitors to explore the creative process behind moving images, from early optical devices to the latest digital technologies.

Notable exhibits at The Museum of the Moving Image include "Behind the Screen," which offers an in-depth look at the production process of film and television, and the "Jim Henson Exhibition," which celebrates the legendary puppeteer and his beloved creations, including the Muppets. The museum also hosts film screenings, panel discussions, and workshops, providing a dynamic and engaging experience for fans of the moving image.

The Museum of the Moving Image Address: 36-01 35th Ave, Astoria, NY 11106

Visiting Hours: Wednesday and Thursday from 10:30 AM to 5:00 PM, Friday from 10:30 AM to 8:00 PM, Saturday and Sunday from 11:30 AM to 6:00 PM. Closed on Monday and Tuesday.

Website: https://www.movingimage.us/

Tickets: General admission is $15 for adults, $11 for seniors (65 and over) and students, and $9 for children (ages 3-17). Admission is free for members and children under 3.

Where to Book: Tickets can be purchased online on the museum's website or in person at the museum's entrance.

Getting There: The nearest subway station is the Steinway Street station on the M and R lines. The Q18 and Q66 buses also stop near the museum.

Tips:

- The museum offers free admission on Fridays from 4:00 PM to 8:00 PM.
- Plan to spend around 2-3 hours exploring the museum's exhibits and screenings.
- Photography is allowed in the museum, but flash photography, tripods, and selfie sticks are not permitted.
- There is an on-site café called Mina's, where you can enjoy a selection of food and beverages.

3.2 Quirky Neighborhoods: DUMBO, Red Hook, and the High Line

New York City is a vibrant patchwork of neighborhoods, each with its unique character and charm. Among the city's countless districts, some stand out for their distinct atmosphere, unusual attractions, and off-the-beaten-path appeal. DUMBO, Red Hook, and the High Line are three such neighborhoods that offer visitors a chance to experience a different side of New York City, away from the typical tourist destinations.

DUMBO

DUMBO, an acronym for "Down Under the Manhattan Bridge Overpass," is a hip, artsy neighborhood nestled between the Manhattan and Brooklyn Bridges in Brooklyn. Once an industrial area, DUMBO has undergone a significant transformation in recent years, becoming a hub for artists, tech startups, and young professionals. The neighborhood's cobblestone streets, historic warehouses, and converted loft spaces create an atmosphere that blends the old and the new.

One of DUMBO's main attractions is the stunning waterfront area, featuring spectacular views of the Manhattan skyline and the iconic Brooklyn Bridge. Visitors can explore Brooklyn Bridge Park, which offers green spaces, walking paths, and various recreational facilities. Art enthusiasts will appreciate the neighborhood's numerous galleries, while foodies can indulge in the diverse culinary offerings, from artisanal bakeries to trendy restaurants.

Red Hook

Red Hook is a quirky, waterfront neighborhood located in southwestern Brooklyn. Known for its industrial past, maritime history, and resilient spirit, Red Hook offers a unique and authentic glimpse of New York City. The neighborhood is characterized by its low-rise buildings, cobbled streets, and stunning views of the Statue of Liberty and the New York Harbor.

Visitors to Red Hook can explore the area's eclectic mix of local shops, bars, and restaurants, many of which are housed in repurposed industrial spaces. Highlights of the neighborhood include the Red Hook Winery, the historic Waterfront Barge Museum, and the Louis Valentino Jr. Park and Pier. Red Hook's isolated location and lack of direct subway access have helped it maintain a distinct, community-driven atmosphere that sets it apart from the rest of the city.

The High Line

The High Line is a unique, elevated public park built on a disused, historic freight rail line on Manhattan's West Side. Stretching from Gansevoort Street in the Meatpacking District to West 34th Street, this 1.45-mile-long greenway offers visitors an oasis of tranquility amidst the city's hustle and bustle. The High Line's innovative design incorporates lush gardens, seating areas, and art installations, making it a popular destination for both locals and tourists.

The park's elevated vantage point provides stunning views of the cityscape, the Hudson River, and the surrounding neighborhoods, including Chelsea and the Meatpacking District. Along the High Line, visitors can explore various attractions, such as the Whitney Museum of American Art, Chelsea Market, and the numerous art galleries that populate the area.

3.3 Secret Gardens: Elevated Acre, 6BC Botanical Garden, and the Lotus Garden

In a city as bustling and energetic as New York, finding a quiet and serene place to relax can be a challenge. However, the city is home to several secret gardens that provide a tranquil haven for those in search of respite from the urban jungle. Elevated Acre, 6BC Botanical Garden, and the Lotus Garden are three such hidden gems that offer visitors an opportunity to experience the city's greener side, away from the well-trodden paths of Central Park and other popular green spaces.

Elevated Acre

Located in the heart of the Financial District, Elevated Acre is a little-known, elevated park that offers a peaceful retreat from the surrounding skyscrapers. Accessible via a hidden escalator on Water Street, this one-acre park sits atop a commercial building, providing visitors with stunning views of the East River, Brooklyn Bridge, and the city's iconic skyline.

Elevated Acre features a beautifully landscaped garden, complete with lush lawns, trees, and a variety of plantings. The park also includes ample seating areas, a small amphitheater, and a wooden boardwalk, making it an ideal spot for a quiet lunch break, a leisurely stroll, or simply taking in the views. Despite its location in one of Manhattan's busiest neighborhoods, Elevated Acre remains a well-kept secret, providing a serene escape from the city's relentless pace.

6BC Botanical Garden

Nestled in the East Village, the 6BC Botanical Garden is a community-run green space that showcases the neighborhood's creative and collaborative spirit. Established in the 1980s on a formerly vacant lot, the garden is now a thriving oasis that features a diverse collection of plants, trees, and flowers, as well as ponds, sculptures, and seating areas.

The 6BC Botanical Garden is maintained by local volunteers and serves as an educational resource for the community, hosting workshops and events related to gardening, sustainability, and the environment. The garden's welcoming atmosphere and lush surroundings make it a perfect spot for relaxation, reflection, and connecting with nature in the heart of the city.

The Lotus Garden

Perched atop a parking garage on Manhattan's Upper West Side, the Lotus Garden is a hidden rooftop garden that offers a serene and enchanting escape from the bustling streets below. Accessed via a discreet entrance on West 97th Street, this community garden features an array of plantings, including lotus flowers, fruit trees, and a vegetable garden.

The Lotus Garden is designed around a central pond, complete with koi fish and aquatic plants, creating a tranquil and calming atmosphere. The garden also includes winding pathways, wooden bridges, and seating areas, allowing visitors to immerse themselves in the peaceful surroundings. Open to the public on Sundays during the warmer months, the Lotus Garden is a well-kept secret and a testament to the power of community collaboration in creating green spaces within the urban environment.

4. Culinary Delights: Diverse Flavors of NYC

4.1 Exploring Manhattan's Food Halls: Chelsea Market, Hudson Yards, and Gansevoort Market

New York City is a culinary paradise, offering a diverse and seemingly endless array of dining options that cater to every palate and budget. In recent years, Manhattan has seen a surge in the popularity of food halls, which bring together a variety of vendors under one roof, providing visitors with a one-stop destination for experiencing the city's vibrant food scene. Chelsea Market, Hudson Yards, and Gansevoort Market are three such food halls that showcase the best of Manhattan's culinary offerings, from classic New York staples to innovative international cuisine.

Chelsea Market

Located in the heart of the Meatpacking District, Chelsea Market is a sprawling, historic food hall that occupies an entire city block. Housed in a former Nabisco factory, this iconic market is a must-visit destination for food lovers, offering an eclectic mix of gourmet shops, artisanal food vendors, and casual eateries.

Visitors to Chelsea Market can indulge in a diverse range of culinary treats, from freshly baked bread and handmade pastries to sushi, tacos, and lobster rolls. Some of the market's standout vendors include Los Tacos No. 1, Doughnuttery, and The Lobster Place. In addition to its food offerings, Chelsea Market also hosts a variety of shops and boutiques, making it an ideal destination for a leisurely afternoon of shopping and dining.

Hudson Yards

Hudson Yards, Manhattan's newest and most ambitious mixed-use development, is home to a cutting-edge food hall that showcases some of the city's most exciting culinary talents. Situated on the West Side, this sleek and modern space features a carefully curated selection of food vendors, ranging from fast-casual eateries to fine dining establishments.

At Hudson Yards, visitors can sample everything from Neapolitan pizza and Spanish tapas to artisanal ice cream and innovative plant-based dishes. Some notable vendors include Mercado Little Spain, a Spanish food market by acclaimed chef José Andrés; Fuku, a fast-casual fried chicken joint by Chef David Chang; and Van Leeuwen, a popular ice cream shop known for its unique flavors. With its diverse food offerings and upscale atmosphere, Hudson Yards provides a contemporary and sophisticated dining experience for visitors to Manhattan.

Gansevoort Market

Gansevoort Market, situated in the heart of the Meatpacking District, is a smaller, more intimate food hall that offers a curated selection of artisanal food vendors and casual eateries. Housed in a historic building with an industrial-chic aesthetic, this market provides a cozy atmosphere that invites visitors to linger and enjoy its culinary delights.

At Gansevoort Market, guests can savor a variety of international cuisine, from authentic Italian fare and Japanese ramen to Middle Eastern dishes and classic American comfort food. Notable vendors include Luzzo's, a Neapolitan pizzeria; The Meatball Guys, which serves up a variety of gourmet meatballs; and Yiaourti, a Greek yogurt bar with an array of sweet and savory toppings. Gansevoort Market's diverse food offerings and inviting ambiance make it a popular destination for both locals and tourists alike.

4.2 Ethnic Enclaves: Little Italy, Chinatown, and Koreatown

New York City is a melting pot of cultures and traditions, and its ethnic enclaves are a testament to the city's rich and diverse heritage. These neighborhoods offer visitors an opportunity to experience the sights, sounds, and tastes of various countries, all within the confines of Manhattan. Little Italy, Chinatown, and Koreatown are three such enclaves that showcase the city's multicultural fabric and provide a unique and immersive cultural experience.

Little Italy

Nestled in the heart of Lower Manhattan, Little Italy is a charming neighborhood steeped in Italian history and culture. Although the area has diminished in size over the years, it continues to be a vibrant destination for those seeking authentic Italian cuisine and a taste of the Old World.

Visitors to Little Italy can wander along the neighborhood's narrow, cobblestone streets, lined with Italian restaurants, cafes, and specialty shops. Some of the area's most famous establishments include Ferrara Bakery & Café, known for its delicious pastries and gelato, and Lombardi's, which claims to be America's first pizzeria. Each September, Little Italy comes alive with the annual Feast of San Gennaro, a lively street fair that celebrates Italian culture with food, music, and entertainment.

Chinatown

Located just south of Little Italy, Manhattan's Chinatown is one of the largest and most vibrant Chinese enclaves in the United States. A bustling hub of activity, Chinatown offers visitors an authentic and immersive experience of Chinese culture, cuisine, and history.

In Chinatown, visitors can explore the neighborhood's numerous shops, selling everything from traditional Chinese herbs and medicine to souvenirs and clothing. The area is also home to a variety of restaurants and food vendors, offering a wide range of Chinese cuisine, from Cantonese dim sum and Sichuan hot pot to hand-pulled noodles and Peking duck. Chinatown's lively atmosphere and colorful streets make it an exciting destination for those seeking to experience a different side of New York City.

Koreatown

Situated in Midtown Manhattan, just a stone's throw away from the Empire State Building, Koreatown is a small but thriving enclave that showcases the best of Korean culture and cuisine. Often referred to as "K-Town," this bustling neighborhood features a dense concentration of Korean restaurants, bars, and shops, all within just a few blocks.

Visitors to Koreatown can indulge in an array of culinary delights, from Korean barbecue and bibimbap to sweet and savory street food. Many of the neighborhood's restaurants are open late into the night, making it a popular destination for both locals and tourists seeking a late-night bite. In addition to its food offerings, K-Town is also known for its karaoke bars, beauty shops, and 24-hour spas, providing visitors with a unique and immersive cultural experience.

4.3 Sustainable Dining: Farm-to-Table Restaurants and Greenmarkets

In recent years, sustainable dining has become increasingly popular in New York City, as residents and visitors alike seek out eco-friendly and health-conscious dining options. Farm-to-table restaurants, which emphasize locally sourced ingredients and a close relationship with producers, are at the forefront of this trend. Additionally, the city's greenmarkets provide shoppers with direct access to fresh, seasonal produce from regional farms. Both options offer a more sustainable and responsible way to enjoy the city's culinary scene while supporting local agriculture and reducing environmental impact.

Farm-to-Table Restaurants

Farm-to-table restaurants in New York City are dedicated to sourcing ingredients from local farmers, artisans, and purveyors, ensuring that their dishes are fresh, seasonal, and sustainable. These establishments not only serve delicious food but also promote a greater awareness of the environmental and social impact of our food choices.

Some noteworthy farm-to-table restaurants in Manhattan include:

1. **Blue Hill:** Located in Greenwich Village, Blue Hill is a renowned farm-to-table restaurant that highlights the flavors of the Hudson Valley. Chef Dan Barber crafts innovative dishes using ingredients from the nearby Blue Hill Farm and other local producers. The restaurant offers a daily-changing menu based on the freshest seasonal ingredients available.

2. **The Little Beet Table:** With a focus on wholesome, vegetable-forward dishes, The Little Beet Table in the Flatiron District serves up a menu that caters to various dietary preferences, including gluten-free, vegetarian, and vegan options. The restaurant sources ingredients from local farms and emphasizes sustainability and seasonality in its culinary offerings.

3. **Loring Place:** Chef Dan Kluger's Loring Place, situated in Greenwich Village, offers a menu inspired by the diverse flavors of New York City and the abundance of the region's local farms. The restaurant's dishes are crafted using fresh, seasonal ingredients, with a strong emphasis on sustainability and supporting local producers.

Greenmarkets

New York City's greenmarkets are another way for locals and visitors to embrace sustainable dining. These farmers' markets provide a direct connection between consumers and regional farmers, offering a wide array of fresh fruits, vegetables, meats, dairy products, and other local goods.

Some popular greenmarkets in Manhattan include:

1. **Union Square Greenmarket:** As one of the city's largest and most famous greenmarkets, the Union Square Greenmarket operates year-round, four days a week. With over 140 regional farmers and producers, this bustling market offers a diverse selection of fresh produce, baked goods, and other local products.

2. **Tompkins Square Greenmarket:** Located in the East Village, the Tompkins Square Greenmarket is a smaller, community-focused market that operates on Sundays. Shoppers can find seasonal produce, artisanal bread, and other local goods from regional farmers and producers.

3. **Columbia University Greenmarket:** Situated in Morningside Heights, the Columbia University Greenmarket operates on Thursdays and

Sundays, providing students and neighborhood residents with access to fresh produce and other local products.

Sustainable dining options like farm-to-table restaurants and greenmarkets offer New Yorkers and visitors alike an opportunity to enjoy the city's culinary scene while supporting local agriculture and minimizing their environmental impact. By embracing these eco-friendly dining options, travelers can indulge in delicious, wholesome food and contribute to a more sustainable future for the city and its inhabitants.

5. Arts and Culture Scene

5.1 Broadway and Beyond: Theater, Musicals, and Off-Broadway

New York City is synonymous with world-class theater, and no trip to Manhattan would be complete without taking in a show. While Broadway is the most famous theater district in the city, boasting an array of spectacular productions and legendary venues, there is much more to New York's theater scene than just Broadway. Off-Broadway and Off-Off-Broadway productions offer a more intimate and experimental theater experience, showcasing an incredible range of talent and creativity.

Broadway

Broadway is the heart of New York City's theater scene and is home to some of the most iconic and celebrated productions in the world. These large-scale productions, known for their elaborate sets, dazzling costumes, and top-notch talent, draw millions of visitors each year.

Some of the most famous Broadway theaters include the **Majestic Theatre**, the **Gershwin Theatre**, and the **Minskoff Theatre**, among many others. Broadway shows often feature well-known performers, both from the theater world and from film and television. Attending a Broadway show is an unforgettable experience, with a range of productions to suit every taste, from classic musicals like "The Phantom of the Opera" and "The Lion King" to contemporary hits like "Hamilton" and "Dear Evan Hansen."

Prices: Ticket prices can vary greatly depending on the show, seating, and availability. Typically, prices range from $30 for balcony or rear mezzanine seats to over $200 for premium orchestra seats. Discounted tickets are sometimes available through services like TKTS or digital lotteries.

Practical Information:

- Booking Tickets: You can purchase tickets online through official ticketing websites like Ticketmaster, Telecharge, or the show's official website. Alternatively, you can buy tickets in person at the theater's box office.

- Last-Minute Tickets: For last-minute or discounted tickets, visit the TKTS booths in Times Square, South Street Seaport, or Lincoln Center. Keep in mind that availability and discounts vary, and tickets are sold on a first-come, first-served basis.

- Rush Tickets: Some theaters offer rush tickets, which are a limited number of discounted tickets sold on the day of the performance. These tickets are usually available when the box office opens, and you may need to arrive early to secure a spot in line.

- Digital Lottery: Many popular shows offer digital lotteries, where you can enter online for a chance to buy discounted tickets. Check the show's official website for information on how to enter.

- Running Time: Most Broadway shows run for about 2-3 hours, including an intermission. Be sure to check the running time of the specific show you're attending.

- Dress Code: While there is no strict dress code for Broadway shows, attendees typically wear smart casual attire. It's best to avoid overly casual clothing like shorts, flip-flops, or tank tops.

- Late Seating: Many theaters have a strict policy on late seating, so it's essential to arrive on time. Latecomers may have to wait for a suitable break in the performance before being allowed to take their seats.

Experience the magic of Broadway and enjoy an unforgettable night of live theater in New York City!

Majestic Theatre

Address: 245 W 44th St, New York, NY 10036

Prices: Ticket prices typically range from $59 to $179.

Website: https://shubert.nyc/theatres/majestic/

Gershwin Theatre

Address: 222 W 51st St, New York, NY 10019

Prices: Ticket prices generally range from $59 to $199.

Website: https://gershwintheatre.com/

Minskoff Theatre

Address: 200 W 45th St, New York, NY 10036

Prices: Ticket prices usually range from $59 to $179.

Website: https://minskofftheatre.boxoffice-tickets.com/

Off-Broadway

For those looking for a more intimate theater experience, Off-Broadway productions offer an excellent alternative to the grandeur of Broadway. Off-Broadway theaters are smaller venues, with a seating capacity between 100 and 499, and often showcase edgier, more innovative works. Off-Broadway productions are known for their high-quality performances and engaging storytelling, and many successful Broadway shows have originated Off-Broadway.

Some well-known Off-Broadway theaters include the **Public Theater**, the **New York Theatre Workshop**, and the **Cherry Lane Theatre**. Popular Off-Broadway productions have included "Avenue Q," "Rent," "Stomp", "Blue Man Group", "Little Shop of Horrors", "The Play That Goes Wrong" and "The 25th Annual Putnam County Spelling Bee." Off-Broadway shows often feature up-and-coming talent and provide an opportunity to see groundbreaking new works before they hit the mainstream.

Prices: Ticket prices for Off-Broadway shows are generally more affordable than Broadway productions. Prices can range from $25 for smaller shows to around $100 for more popular productions. Discounts are often available through various ticketing services.

Practical Information:

- Booking Tickets: Tickets for Off-Broadway shows can be purchased online through ticketing websites like Ticketmaster or the show's official website. You can also buy tickets in person at the theater's box office.

- Last-Minute Tickets: Discounted tickets for Off-Broadway shows can often be found at the TKTS booths in Times Square, South Street Seaport, and Lincoln Center. Availability and discounts vary, and tickets are sold on a first-come, first-served basis.

- Rush Tickets: Some Off-Broadway theaters offer rush tickets, which are a limited number of discounted tickets sold on the day of the performance. These tickets are usually available when the box office opens, and you may need to arrive early to secure a spot in line.

- Running Time: The running time for Off-Broadway shows can vary, but most performances run for about 1.5-2.5 hours, often with an intermission. Check the running time of the specific show you're attending.

- Dress Code: There is no strict dress code for Off-Broadway shows, but smart casual attire is generally the norm. It's best to avoid overly casual clothing like shorts, flip-flops, or tank tops.

- Late Seating: Off-Broadway theaters may have different policies regarding late seating. It's always a good idea to arrive on time to avoid any issues.

Public Theater

Address: 425 Lafayette St, New York, NY 10003| Prices: Ticket prices typically range from $20 to $95 | Website: https://publictheater.org/

New York Theatre Workshop

Address: 79 E 4th St, New York, NY 10003| Prices: Ticket prices generally range from $30 to $65, with discounts available for students and seniors.| Website: https://www.nytw.org/

Cherry Lane Theatre

Address: 38 Commerce St, New York, NY 10014| Prices: Ticket prices usually range from $25 to $65 | https://www.cherrylanetheatre.org/

Off-Off-Broadway

Off-Off-Broadway is the most experimental and avant-garde tier of New York City's theater scene. These productions take place in venues with fewer than 100 seats and often have limited budgets. However, what they lack in financial resources, they make up for in creativity and artistic ambition.

Off-Off-Broadway theaters, such as **La MaMa**, **The Flea Theater**, and **Dixon Place**, offer an opportunity to see daring and unconventional works that push the boundaries of traditional theater. While these productions may not have the glitz and glamour of Broadway, they provide a unique and immersive experience for theatergoers seeking something out of the ordinary.

La MaMa

Address: 66 E 4th St, New York, NY 10003 | Prices: Ticket prices typically range from $10 to $30.| Website: https://lamama.org/

The Flea Theater

Address: 20 Thomas St, New York, NY 10007 | Prices: Ticket prices usually range from $15 to $35| Website: https://theflea.org/

Dixon Place

Address: 161A Chrystie St, New York, NY 10002 | Prices: Ticket prices generally vary from $10 to $25, with some events being free | Website: http://dixonplace.org/

5.2 Live Music Venues: Jazz, Indie Rock, and Classical

New York City boasts a vibrant and eclectic live music scene, with venues catering to every genre and taste. From historic jazz clubs to cutting-edge indie rock spaces and world-class classical concert halls, Manhattan has something for every music lover. Here are some notable venues for jazz, indie rock, and classical music, along with their websites, addresses, and general price ranges:

Jazz

1. Blue Note is a legendary jazz club in the heart of Greenwich Village. Since 1981, it has hosted performances by some of the most iconic names in jazz, including Dizzy Gillespie, Sarah Vaughan, and Oscar Peterson. The intimate setting and top-notch talent make it a must-visit destination for jazz enthusiasts.

Blue Note

Website: https://www.bluenotejazz.com/newyork/ |Address: 131 W 3rd St, New York, NY 10012| Price range: $20 - $65 (depending on the artist and seating)

2. **The Village Vanguard**, opened in 1935, is one of the oldest and most celebrated jazz clubs in the world. This intimate venue has played host to a who's who of jazz greats, such as John Coltrane, Bill Evans, and Thelonious Monk. The club's storied history and exceptional acoustics make it a bucket-list destination for jazz lovers.

Village Vanguard

Website: https://www.villagevanguard.com/ |Address: 178 7th Ave S, New York, NY 10014 |Price range: $35 - $50 (plus a one-drink minimum)

Indie Rock

1. The **Bowery Ballroom** is a popular indie rock venue located in the Lower East Side. With a capacity of around 600, this intimate space offers excellent sightlines and acoustics, making it a favorite among both performers and audiences. The Bowery Ballroom showcases a diverse array of up-and-coming and established indie rock acts.

Bowery Ballroom Website: https://www.boweryballroom.com/ | Address: 6 Delancey St, New York, NY 10002 | Price range: $15 - $40 (depending on the artist)

2. The **Mercury Lounge**, also in the Lower East Side, is a smaller venue known for hosting early performances by notable indie rock bands, such as The Strokes and Interpol. With a capacity of around 250, this cozy space provides an up-close-and-personal live music experience, featuring a mix of local talent and touring acts.

Mercury Lounge

Website: https://www.mercuryeastpresents.com/mercurylounge |Address: 217 E Houston St, New York, NY 10002| Price range: $10 - $25 (depending on the artist)

Classical

1. **Carnegie Hall** is one of the most prestigious classical music venues in the world. Since its opening in 1891, it has hosted performances by legendary musicians, such as Tchaikovsky, Leonard Bernstein, and Yo-Yo Ma. The hall's stunning architecture and exceptional acoustics make it an unforgettable destination for classical music aficionados.

Carnegie Hall

Website: https://www.carnegiehall.org/ |Address: 881 Seventh Ave, New York, NY 10019 |Price range: $20 - $200+ (depending on the event and seating)

2. **Lincoln Center** is a world-class performing arts complex that hosts a variety of classical music events, including performances by the New York Philharmonic, the Metropolitan Opera, and the Chamber Music Society of Lincoln Center. The complex features several stunning venues, such as David Geffen Hall, the Metropolitan Opera House, and Alice Tully Hall, each with its own unique ambiance and architectural features.

Lincoln Center for the Performing Arts

Website: https://www.lincolncenter.org/ |Address: 10 Lincoln Center Plaza, New York, NY 10023 |Price range: $30 - $300+ (depending on the event and seating)

5.3 Film Festivals and Independent Cinemas

New York City is a hub for the film industry, with a rich history of movie-making and film appreciation. The city is home to numerous film festivals and independent cinemas that showcase a diverse range of films from all over the world, providing audiences with unique opportunities to explore cinema beyond the mainstream Hollywood fare.

Film Festivals

1. **Tribeca Film Festival** - https://www.tribecafilm.com/

The Tribeca Film Festival, founded by Robert De Niro, Jane Rosenthal, and Craig Hatkoff in 2002, is one of the most prominent film festivals in the world. Held annually in the spring, the festival showcases a vast array of feature films, documentaries, shorts, and immersive storytelling experiences. In addition to film screenings, the festival also hosts panel discussions, workshops, and live music events, making it a must-attend event for film enthusiasts.

2. **New York Film Festival** - https://www.filmlinc.org/nyff/

The New York Film Festival, organized by the Film Society of Lincoln Center, has been a fixture of the city's cinematic landscape since 1963. This prestigious festival takes place in the fall and features a carefully curated selection of international films, including world premieres, retrospectives, and documentaries. The festival is also known for its in-depth discussions and masterclasses with renowned filmmakers and industry professionals.

3. **DOC NYC**- https://www.docnyc.net/

DOC NYC is America's largest documentary film festival and takes place annually in November. The festival showcases a wide variety of documentary films, including features, shorts, and works-in-progress. In addition to screenings, DOC NYC offers panels, workshops, and networking events, making it an essential destination for documentary filmmakers and fans alike.

Independent Cinemas

1. Film Forum

Website: https://filmforum.org/ | Address: 209 W Houston St, New York, NY 10014

Film Forum is a nonprofit, independent movie theater located in the West Village. It is dedicated to showcasing independent, foreign, and classic films that are often overlooked by mainstream theaters. With a robust calendar of new releases, repertory films, and special events, Film Forum is an essential destination for cinephiles in search of thought-provoking and artful cinema.

2. IFC Center

Website: https://www.ifccenter.com/ | Address: 323 6th Ave, New York, NY 10014

The IFC Center, located in Greenwich Village, is another popular independent cinema known for screening a diverse selection of films, including foreign, documentary, and independent features. The theater also hosts special events, such as filmmaker Q&As and midnight screenings of cult classics, providing a unique and engaging movie-going experience.

3. Angelika Film Center

Website: https://www.angelikafilmcenter.com/nyc | Address: 18 W Houston St, New York, NY 10012

The Angelika Film Center, situated in the heart of SoHo, is a stylish and intimate cinema that specializes in showcasing independent and foreign films. With its cozy atmosphere and carefully curated programming, the Angelika offers audiences an opportunity to discover hidden gems and engage with a diverse range of cinematic voices.

6. Sports and Recreation

6.1 Major Sports Teams: Yankees, Mets, Knicks, and Rangers

New York City is a sports lover's paradise, with a wide range of professional sports teams that inspire passionate fan bases and create memorable experiences. Four of the city's most iconic teams are the New York Yankees and New York Mets (Major League Baseball), the New York Knicks (National Basketball Association), and the New York Rangers (National Hockey League). Each of these teams has a storied history and a dedicated following that contributes to the city's vibrant sports culture.

New York Yankee https://www.mlb.com/yankees

The New York Yankees, founded in 1901, are one of the most successful and well-known professional sports franchises in the world. With a record 27 World Series championships, the Yankees have established a winning tradition that has made them a symbol of excellence in baseball. The team's home games are played at the iconic Yankee Stadium in the Bronx, which is known for its electric atmosphere and rich history. Attending a Yankees game is a quintessential New York City experience, complete with the famous "roll call" by the Bleacher Creatures and the chance to witness history in the making.

New York Yankees ticket prices can vary greatly depending on several factors such as the opponent, day of the week, seat location, and time of the season.

On average, ticket prices for a regular season New York Yankees game range from around $20 for the most affordable seats in the upper levels to over $300 for premium seating areas like the Legends Suite or Delta Sky360 Suite. However, some tickets can be found at even lower prices during promotional events or for less popular games.

Keep in mind that prices may fluctuate due to demand, and purchasing tickets well in advance or using ticket resale websites may result in better deals. It's always a good idea to check the New York Yankees' official website or reputable ticket platforms for the most up-to-date pricing information.

New York Mets https://www.mlb.com/mets

The New York Mets, founded in 1962, are another Major League Baseball team that calls the city home. The Mets play their home games at Citi Field in Queens, a modern ballpark with a nod to the team's history and New York's baseball heritage. Although the team has experienced its share of ups and downs, the Mets have a loyal fan base that passionately supports them through thick and thin. Attending a Mets game offers a fun and family-friendly atmosphere, complete with Mr. Met, one of the most beloved mascots in professional sports.

New York Knicks- https://www.nba.com/knicks

The New York Knicks, founded in 1946, are a professional basketball team in the National Basketball Association (NBA). The team plays its home games at the world-famous Madison Square Garden, located in the heart of Manhattan. While the Knicks have experienced varying levels of success throughout their history, the team remains one of the most iconic franchises in the NBA. Attending a Knicks game offers an exciting and high-energy experience, complete with celebrity sightings, passionate fans, and the chance to watch elite athletes compete on the sport's biggest stage.

New York Rangers https://www.nhl.com/rangers

The New York Rangers, founded in 1926, are a professional ice hockey team in the National Hockey League (NHL). Like the Knicks, the Rangers play their home games at Madison Square Garden. As one of the NHL's "Original Six" franchises, the team has a long and storied history, with four Stanley Cup championships to their name. Rangers games are known for their intense, fast-paced action and the enthusiastic fan base that fills the Garden with energy and excitement. Attending a Rangers game offers a thrilling and unique sports experience that is quintessentially New York.

6.2 Alternative Sports Activities: Indoor Rock Climbing, Paddleboarding, and Biking

New York City offers a wide range of alternative sports activities for both residents and visitors looking for a more unique and adventurous experience. These activities provide excellent opportunities for exercise, exploration, and fun outside of traditional sports. Some popular alternative sports activities in the city include indoor rock climbing, paddleboarding, and biking.

Indoor Rock Climbing

Indoor rock climbing is a popular activity in New York City that allows people to challenge themselves physically and mentally while enjoying a fun workout. Several indoor climbing gyms cater to various skill levels, from beginners to seasoned climbers. Here are a couple of notable climbing gyms in Manhattan:

1. **The Cliffs at LIC**

https://lic.thecliffsclimbing.com/ |Address: 11-11 44th Dr, Long Island City, NY 11101

The Cliffs at LIC, located in Long Island City, offers a massive indoor climbing space with bouldering, top-rope, and lead climbing options. The gym provides climbing classes, private instruction, and youth programs, making it suitable for all ages and skill levels.

2. **Brooklyn Boulders**

Website: https://brooklynboulders.com/ |Address: 575 Degraw St, Brooklyn, NY 11217

Brooklyn Boulders, located in the Gowanus neighborhood of Brooklyn, features extensive bouldering walls, top-rope climbing, and fitness facilities. The gym offers climbing courses, yoga classes, and events, creating a vibrant and supportive community for climbers of all abilities.

Paddleboarding

Paddleboarding is an excellent way to explore New York City's waterways while enjoying a full-body workout. Several outfitters offer stand-up paddleboarding (SUP) lessons, rentals, and guided tours along the Hudson River, East River, and other waterways.

1. **Manhattan Kayak**

Website: https://manhattankayak.com/ | Address: Pier 84 Boathouse, W 44th St & 12th Ave, New York, NY 10036

Manhattan Kayak, located at Pier 84 on the Hudson River, offers SUP lessons, rentals, and guided tours. Paddle along the Hudson River and take in the spectacular views of the Manhattan skyline, all while getting a great workout on the water.

Biking

Biking is a popular and eco-friendly way to explore the city, with numerous bike lanes, parks, and trails offering safe and scenic routes. Renting a bike is easy, with several rental options available throughout the city.

1. **Citi Bike**

Website: https://www.citibikenyc.com/

Citi Bike is New York City's bike-sharing system, with thousands of bikes available at docking stations throughout Manhattan, Brooklyn, Queens, and the Bronx. Users can rent a bike for a single ride, or purchase a day pass or monthly membership for unlimited access to the bikes.

2. **Central Park Bike Rentals**

Website: https://www.centralparknyc.org/activities/biking

Central Park, with its numerous bike paths and scenic beauty, is a popular destination for cyclists. Several rental companies, such as Bike Rental Central Park and Unlimited Biking, offer hourly and daily bike rentals to explore the park's 843 acres of green space

Prices for bike rentals can vary depending on the rental duration and any additional services or equipment you may require. Here are some general price estimates for Central Park Bike Rentals:

- 1 hour: $10 - $15
- 2 hours: $15 - $20
- 3 hours: $20 - $25
- 4 hours: $25 - $30
- Full day (up to 24 hours): $40 - $50

These prices typically include a helmet, lock, and a map of Central Park. Additional services or equipment, such as tandem bikes, baby seats, or guided tours, may come with an extra cost. It's always a good idea to check the specific bike rental company's website for the most up-to-date pricing information and to make reservations in advance to ensure availability.

Some popular bike rental companies in Central Park include:

- Central Park Sightseeing: https://www.centralparksightseeing.com/
- Bike Rental Central Park: https://www.bikerentalcentralpark.com/
- Unlimited Biking: https://www.unlimitedbiking.com/central-park-bike-rental/

6.3 Parks and Green Spaces: Prospect Park, Battery Park, and Riverside Park

New York City is home to numerous parks and green spaces that offer residents and visitors a welcome respite from the urban hustle and bustle. These spaces provide opportunities for relaxation, recreation, and enjoyment of the city's natural beauty. While Central Park is the most famous park in the city, there are many other noteworthy green spaces, including Prospect Park, Battery Park, and Riverside Park.

Prospect Park

Website: https://www.prospectpark.org/ | Address: Brooklyn, NY 11225

Designed by the same landscape architects who created Central Park, Frederick Law Olmsted and Calvert Vaux, Prospect Park is a 585-acre oasis located in the heart of Brooklyn. The park features a picturesque 90-acre Long Meadow, the 60-acre lake, and the only remaining forest in Brooklyn. There are numerous walking and biking paths, sports fields, playgrounds, and even a historic carousel. The park also hosts events like outdoor concerts, food festivals, and greenmarkets. The Prospect Park Zoo, the LeFrak Center at Lakeside, and the Brooklyn Botanic Garden are additional attractions within or adjacent to the park.

Battery Park

Website: https://www.thebattery.org/ | Address: Battery Pl, State St and Whitehall St, New York, NY 10004

Located at the southern tip of Manhattan, Battery Park is a 25-acre public park that offers stunning views of the Statue of Liberty, Ellis Island, and New York Harbor. The park features beautiful gardens, waterfront promenades, and plenty of seating areas, making it an ideal spot for relaxation and sightseeing. Battery Park is also home to the historic Castle Clinton, which now serves as the ticket office for the Statue of Liberty and Ellis Island ferries. Additionally, the park hosts outdoor concerts, art installations, and other events throughout the year.

Riverside Park

Website: https://riversideparknyc.org/ | Address: Riverside Dr To Hudson River, W 59 St To Clair Pl, New York, NY 10069

Stretching over four miles along the Hudson River, Riverside Park is a scenic green space on Manhattan's Upper West Side. The park, designed by Frederick Law Olmsted in the 1870s, offers a variety of recreational opportunities, including walking and biking paths, playgrounds, sports fields, and dog runs. The park also features beautiful gardens, monuments, and public art installations. A popular attraction within the park is the General Grant National Memorial, the final resting place of Ulysses S. Grant, the 18th President of the United States. Riverside Park is also home to the Summer on the Hudson event series, which includes free concerts, movies, and other outdoor activities.

7. Shopping in Manhattan

7.1 Luxury Boutiques: Fifth Avenue, Madison Avenue, and SoHo

New York City is a global fashion capital, renowned for its luxury shopping experiences and iconic retail destinations. For those looking to indulge in high-end retail therapy, the city offers a wealth of luxury boutiques and designer stores. Three of the most famous shopping districts in New York City are Fifth Avenue, Madison Avenue, and SoHo, each providing a unique and upscale shopping experience.

Fifth Avenue

Address: Fifth Avenue, from 42nd Street to 60th Street, New York, NY

Fifth Avenue, located in the heart of Manhattan, is one of the world's most famous shopping streets. Known for its prestigious retail stores and luxury boutiques, Fifth Avenue attracts shoppers from around the globe. Along this iconic street, you'll find flagship stores for some of the biggest names in fashion, such as Bergdorf Goodman, Tiffany & Co., Gucci, and Louis Vuitton. Additionally, Fifth Avenue is home to the famous Saks Fifth Avenue department store, which offers an extensive selection of designer clothing, accessories, and beauty products. With its elegant window displays and upscale atmosphere, Fifth Avenue is a must-visit destination for luxury shopping in New York City.

Madison Avenue

Address: Madison Avenue, from 57th Street to 72nd Street, New York, NY

Madison Avenue, situated on Manhattan's Upper East Side, is another iconic shopping destination, known for its luxury boutiques and high-end designer stores. This elegant avenue features a more intimate and exclusive shopping experience compared to the bustling Fifth Avenue. Along Madison Avenue, you'll find flagship stores for prominent fashion houses like Chanel, Hermès, Tom Ford, and Dolce & Gabbana, as well as exclusive jewelers such as Bvlgari and David Yurman. The refined atmosphere and prestigious retailers make Madison Avenue an ideal destination for those seeking a sophisticated shopping experience.

SoHo

Address: SoHo District, New York, NY

SoHo, short for "South of Houston Street," is a trendy neighborhood in lower Manhattan known for its historic cast-iron architecture, cobblestone streets, and upscale shopping scene. This fashionable district offers a unique mix of luxury boutiques, contemporary designer stores, and cutting-edge art galleries. SoHo is home to flagship stores for many high-end designers, including Saint Laurent, Alexander Wang, and Isabel Marant, as well as popular fashion brands like Prada, Versace, and Stella McCartney. In addition to its luxury retailers, SoHo is also famous for its chic boutiques and concept stores, such as Opening Ceremony and The Webster, which showcase emerging designers and limited-edition collections. SoHo's eclectic mix of high-end fashion, art, and dining make it a vibrant and stylish destination for luxury shopping in New York City.

7.2 Unique Local Shops and Independent Designers

While New York City is known for its luxury boutiques and high-end shopping districts, the city is also a haven for unique local shops and independent designers. These stores offer an opportunity to discover one-of-a-kind items, support local artisans, and experience the city's diverse creative scene. Here are some notable independent shops and designers worth exploring in New York City:

1. **Catbird**

Catbird is a jewelry boutique that specializes in delicate, handmade pieces from local designers. Catbird has become a go-to destination for fashionistas seeking unique and ethically sourced jewelry, including engagement rings, necklaces, bracelets, and earrings.

https://www.catbirdnyc.com/ |Address: 219 Bedford Ave, Brooklyn, NY 11211 Located in the heart of Williamsburg,

2. **McNally Jackson Books**

McNally Jackson Books is an independent bookstore located in SoHo, offering a carefully curated selection of fiction, non-fiction, and art books. The store also features a cozy café, regular author events, and a unique selection of stationery and gifts, making it a favorite among book lovers and a staple in the local community.

Website: https://www.mcnallyjackson.com/ |Address: 52 Prince St, New York, NY 10012

3. **Swords-Smith**

Swords-Smith is a contemporary boutique in Williamsburg, Brooklyn, that showcases emerging and independent fashion designers from around the world. This stylish store offers a wide range of clothing, accessories, and jewelry for men and women, providing a unique shopping experience for those seeking innovative and original designs.

Website: https://swords-smith.com/ |Address: 98 S 4th St, Brooklyn, NY 11249

4. **Fishs Eddy:**

Fishs Eddy is a quirky and beloved home goods store near Union Square in Manhattan. This shop is famous for its vintage-inspired dishware, glassware, and kitchen accessories, which feature whimsical designs and illustrations. Fishs Eddy is the perfect place to find unique gifts and conversation-starting pieces for your home.

Website: https://www.fishseddy.com/ |Address: 889 Broadway, New York, NY 10003

5. **Strand Bookstore**

The Strand Bookstore, located near Union Square, is an iconic New York City institution known for its extensive selection of new, used, and rare books. This independent bookstore boasts over 18 miles of books, with a vast array of genres and titles to choose from. The Strand is a must-visit destination for book lovers and those seeking a quintessential New York City experience.

Website: https://www.strandbooks.com/| Address: 828 Broadway, New York, NY 10003

6. Dover Street Market

Dover Street Market, located in Midtown Manhattan, is a multi-brand retail space that showcases cutting-edge fashion and independent designers. This innovative concept store features an eclectic mix of established and emerging fashion brands, as well as a curated selection of art, accessories, and home goods.

Website: https://www.doverstreetmarket.com/ |Address: 160 Lexington Ave, New York, NY 10016

7.3 Vintage and Thrift Stores: The Ultimate Guide

New York City is a treasure trove for vintage and thrift store enthusiasts. These shops offer a diverse array of clothing, accessories, and home goods, giving shoppers the chance to find unique, high-quality items at affordable prices. Whether you're a seasoned thrifter or new to the scene, this ultimate guide to New York City's vintage and thrift stores will help you discover the best spots for scoring one-of-a-kind treasures.

1. Beacon's Closet

Website: https://www.beaconscloset.com/ |Addresses: Multiple locations in Brooklyn and Manhattan

Beacon's Closet is a popular chain of vintage and thrift stores with locations in Brooklyn and Manhattan. Known for its vast selection of clothing, shoes, and accessories for men and women, Beacon's Closet offers an extensive range of styles, from designer labels to unique vintage finds. With a constant influx of new inventory, shoppers are sure to find something special at Beacon's Closet.

2. **Housing Works Thrift Shops**

Website: https://www.housingworks.org/locations/category/thrift-shops |Addresses: Multiple locations throughout Manhattan and Brooklyn

Housing Works is a non-profit organization with thrift shops throughout New York City. These stores offer a curated selection of clothing, furniture, and home goods, with proceeds supporting the organization's mission to end homelessness and AIDS. In addition to finding great deals on gently used items, shoppers can feel good about supporting a worthy cause.

3. **L Train Vintage**

Website: http://ltrainvintage.com/ |Addresses: Multiple locations in Brooklyn

L Train Vintage is a popular chain of thrift stores with locations throughout Brooklyn. Known for its affordable prices and eclectic selection, L Train Vintage offers a wide range of clothing and accessories for men and women. From vintage band tees to unique denim finds, L Train Vintage is a must-visit destination for thrifters seeking great deals on unique items.

4. **The Break**

Website: https://www.shopthebreak.com/ |Address: 82 Dobbin St, Brooklyn, NY 11222

The Break, located in Greenpoint, Brooklyn, is a stylish vintage store offering a curated selection of clothing, accessories, and home goods. With a focus on sustainable fashion, The Break provides shoppers with affordable, on-trend pieces that reflect the store's commitment to quality and style.

5. 10 ft Single by Stella Dallas

Address: 285 N 6th St, Brooklyn, NY 11211

10 ft Single by Stella Dallas is a beloved vintage store located in Williamsburg, Brooklyn. The shop offers a wide range of vintage clothing and accessories, with an emphasis on items from the 1950s to the 1990s. With its well-organized inventory and affordable prices, 10 ft Single is a favorite among vintage enthusiasts and casual shoppers alike.

6. Mr. Throwback

Website: https://mrthrowback.com/ Address: 428 E 9th St, New York, NY 10009

Located in Manhattan's East Village, Mr. Throwback is a one-of-a-kind vintage store specializing in nostalgic sports apparel and memorabilia. From jerseys and jackets to snapbacks and sneakers, Mr. Throwback offers an impressive selection of retro sports gear that's sure to delight fans and collectors.

7. No Relation Vintage

Website: https://ltrainvintagenyc.com/ |Address: 204 1st Avenue, New York, NY 10009

No Relation Vintage, part of the L Train Vintage family, is a popular vintage and thrift store located in Manhattan's East Village. The shop offers a wide selection of clothing and accessories for men and women, with an emphasis on affordable prices and unique finds. From classic denim jackets to vintage dresses, No Relation Vintage has something for everyone.

8. Awoke Vintage

Website: https://www.awokevintage.com/ |Addresses: Multiple locations in Brooklyn

Awoke Vintage is a trendy vintage clothing store with locations in Williamsburg and Greenpoint, Brooklyn. This boutique offers a curated selection of clothing and accessories for men and women, with an emphasis on unique, high-quality pieces. Awoke Vintage is a great destination for fashion-forward shoppers seeking stylish vintage finds.

9. Buffalo Exchange

Website: https://www.buffaloexchange.com/ |Addresses: Multiple locations in Manhattan and Brooklyn

Buffalo Exchange is a popular buy-sell-trade clothing store with locations in Manhattan and Brooklyn. This thrift store offers a wide range of clothing and accessories for men and women, with a focus on contemporary styles and designer labels. At Buffalo Exchange, shoppers can find great deals on gently used items while also trading in their own clothes for cash or store credit.

10. East Village Vintage Collective

Website: https://www.eastvillagevintagecollective.com/| Address: 545 E 12th St, New York, NY 10009

East Village Vintage Collective, located in Manhattan's East Village, is a cozy vintage store offering a carefully curated selection of clothing, accessories, and home goods. This shop is known for its diverse range of styles, from classic vintage pieces to quirky, one-of-a-kind finds. East Village Vintage Collective is an excellent destination for those looking to explore the city's unique vintage scene.

8. Nightlife and Entertainment

8.1 Rooftop Bars with Stunning Views

New York City is famous for its awe-inspiring skyline, and there's no better way to experience it than from a rooftop bar. These elevated venues offer a unique perspective on the city while providing the perfect setting for enjoying delicious food, innovative cocktails, and good company. Here are some of the most stunning rooftop bars in New York City, each offering unparalleled views and memorable experiences:

1. **230 Fifth Rooftop Bar**

Website: https://www.230-fifth.com/ Address: 230 5th Ave, New York, NY 10001

Located in the heart of Manhattan, 230 Fifth Rooftop Bar boasts breathtaking views of the Empire State Building and the surrounding skyline. The spacious open-air bar offers comfortable seating, seasonal events, and a delicious food and drink menu. Don't miss their signature cocktails and cozy igloos during the winter months.

2. **The Press Lounge**

Website: https://www.thepresslounge.com/ |Address: 653 11th Ave, New York, NY 10036

Perched atop the Kimpton Ink48 Hotel in Hell's Kitchen, The Press Lounge offers panoramic views of the Hudson River and the Manhattan skyline. This sophisticated venue features a stylish interior, outdoor seating, and an extensive drink menu, making it an ideal spot for a special night out or a relaxing evening with friends.

3. **Le Bain**

Website: https://www.standardhotels.com/new-york/features/le-bain
Address: The Standard, High Line, 848 Washington St, New York, NY 10014

Le Bain, located at The Standard High Line Hotel in the Meatpacking District, is a chic rooftop bar with stunning views of the Hudson River and the city skyline. Known for its vibrant atmosphere, Le Bain offers a plunge pool, dance floor, and an expansive outdoor terrace. Enjoy their signature cocktails and light bites as you take in the city's breathtaking scenery.

4. **Westlight**

Website: https://www.westlightnyc.com/ |Address: 111 N 12th St, Brooklyn, NY 11249

Situated atop The William Vale Hotel in Williamsburg, Brooklyn, Westlight offers a spectacular view of Manhattan's skyline and the East River. This stylish rooftop bar features floor-to-ceiling windows, comfortable seating, and a creative cocktail menu designed by acclaimed mixologist Anne Robinson. Sample their globally inspired small plates while soaking in the incredible vistas.

5. **Refinery Rooftop**

Website: https://www.refineryrooftopnyc.com/| Address: 63 W 38th St, New York, NY 10018

Nestled in the Garment District, Refinery Rooftop offers an industrial-chic ambiance with stunning views of the Empire State Building. The rooftop bar, located at the Refinery Hotel, features both indoor and outdoor seating areas, a retractable glass roof, and a menu of inventive cocktails and American cuisine. The cozy atmosphere and iconic views make Refinery Rooftop a must-visit destination.

6. **Bar SixtyFive**

Website: https://www.rainbowroom.com/bar-sixty-five |Address: 30 Rockefeller Plaza, 65th Floor, New York, NY 10112

Bar SixtyFive, situated on the 65th floor of 30 Rockefeller Plaza, offers an upscale experience with spectacular views of the city. This elegant rooftop bar, located just one floor below the iconic Rainbow Room, features a stylish Art Deco-inspired interior and an outdoor terrace. Enjoy their classic cocktails, extensive wine list, and gourmet bar bites while marveling at the panoramic views.

8.2 Speakeasies and Hidden Bars: Prohibition-Era Glamour

New York City's speakeasies and hidden bars offer a glimpse into the city's Prohibition-era past while providing a unique and intimate atmosphere for enjoying cocktails and conversation. These clandestine watering holes, often disguised behind unmarked doors or secret entrances, evoke the glamour and intrigue of the 1920s. Here are some of the most noteworthy speakeasies and hidden bars in New York City, where you can step back in time and savor the allure of Prohibition-era glamour:

1. **PDT (Please Don't Tell)**

Website: https://www.pdtnyc.com/ |Address: 113 St Marks Pl, New York, NY 10009

PDT, short for Please Don't Tell, is a modern speakeasy located behind a hidden door inside Crif Dogs, a popular hot dog joint in the East Village. Accessible through a vintage phone booth, this intimate bar is known for its inventive cocktails, cozy ambiance, and exclusive vibe. Reservations are recommended, as space is limited.

2. **Bathtub Gin**

Website: https://www.bathtubginnyc.com/| Address: 132 9th Ave, New York, NY 10011

Hidden behind a secret door in a Chelsea coffee shop, Bathtub Gin offers a Prohibition-era experience complete with an actual copper bathtub at its center. The dimly lit space features plush banquettes, live jazz, and burlesque performances. Sip on expertly crafted cocktails, including their signature gin-based concoctions, while soaking in the speakeasy atmosphere.

3. **Apothéke**

Website: https://www.apothekenyc.com/ Address: 9 Doyers St, New York, NY 10013

Apothéke, tucked away on a narrow street in Chinatown, is a hidden gem inspired by European apothecaries. This upscale cocktail bar, accessible through an unmarked door, features a menu of "prescription" cocktails crafted from exotic ingredients and house-made tinctures. The elegant, candlelit setting and live music make Apothéke a perfect destination for a romantic night out.

4. **The Back Room**

Website: http://www.backroomnyc.com/ Address: 102 Norfolk St, New York, NY 10002

The Back Room, located on the Lower East Side, is one of the few remaining original speakeasies from the Prohibition era. To enter, you'll need to navigate through a hidden door and a narrow alleyway. The bar maintains its authentic atmosphere with velvet wallpaper, vintage furniture, and cocktails served in teacups. Experience a piece of New York City history while enjoying live jazz and classic libations.

5. **Attaboy**

Address: 134 Eldridge St, New York, NY 10002

Attaboy, situated in the Lower East Side, is a hidden bar housed in the former location of the legendary Milk & Honey speakeasy. With no menu, the expert bartenders at Attaboy craft bespoke cocktails based on your preferences, creating a personalized and unforgettable experience. The unmarked entrance and minimalist decor add to the allure of this modern speakeasy.

6. **Angel's Share**

Address: 8 Stuyvesant St, New York, NY 10003

Hidden inside a Japanese restaurant in the East Village, Angel's Share is an elegant, unmarked bar known for its innovative cocktails and serene atmosphere. With a strict no-standing policy, this intimate speakeasy offers a relaxed and quiet setting for savoring expertly crafted drinks and small plates.

8.3 Comedy Clubs and Cabaret Shows

New York City has long been a hub for live entertainment, and its comedy clubs and cabaret shows are no exception. From world-class stand-up comedians to captivating theatrical performances, these venues offer a variety of experiences that showcase the city's vibrant and diverse performing arts scene. Here are some of the most popular comedy clubs and cabaret shows in New York City, where you can enjoy a night filled with laughter, music, and unforgettable performances:

1. **Comedy Cellar**

Website: https://www.comedycellar.com/ Address: 117 Macdougal St, New York, NY 10012

The Comedy Cellar, located in Greenwich Village, is one of the most iconic comedy clubs in the world. Known for hosting top-notch comedians and surprise appearances by famous performers like Jerry Seinfeld, Chris Rock, and Amy Schumer, this intimate venue offers multiple shows every night, with a diverse lineup of stand-up acts.

2. **Carolines on Broadway**

Website: https://www.carolines.com/ Address: 1626 Broadway, New York, NY 10019

Carolines on Broadway is a legendary comedy club situated in the heart of Times Square. This upscale venue hosts some of the biggest names in comedy, as well as up-and-coming talents. With a full-service restaurant and bar, Carolines offers a complete night of entertainment, featuring high-quality acts in a stylish setting.

3. **Gotham Comedy Club**

Website: https://www.gothamcomedyclub.com/ Address: 208 W 23rd St, New York, NY 10011

Gotham Comedy Club, located in Chelsea, is a renowned venue that has hosted some of the biggest names in comedy, including Dave Chappelle, Jim Gaffigan, and Ellen DeGeneres. This modern club offers a comfortable, intimate atmosphere with excellent sightlines and a diverse lineup of comedians, making it a top destination for comedy fans.

4. **Joe's Pub**

Website: https://www.publictheater.org/programs--events/joes-pub/ Address: 425 Lafayette St, New York, NY 10003

Joe's Pub, part of The Public Theater in NoHo, is a celebrated venue for cabaret, music, and theater performances. This intimate, 190-seat space features a diverse range of shows, including everything from emerging artists to Broadway stars. With a full dinner menu and extensive drink options, Joe's Pub offers a unique and sophisticated night of entertainment.

5. **54 Below**

Website: https://54below.com/ Address: 254 W 54th St, Cellar, New York, NY 10019

54 Below, also known as Feinstein's/54 Below, is a premier cabaret and supper club located in the basement of the iconic Studio 54. This intimate venue showcases Broadway's brightest stars, as well as up-and-coming talents, in a variety of musical and theatrical performances. The elegant setting, complete with fine dining and expertly crafted cocktails, makes 54 Below a must-visit destination for fans of live entertainment.

6. **The Duplex**

Website: https://www.theduplex.com/ Address: 61 Christopher St, New York, NY 10014

The Duplex, situated in Greenwich Village, is a historic cabaret and piano bar that has been a staple of the New York City nightlife scene since 1950. This two-story venue features a diverse lineup of performers, from drag queens to singer-songwriters, and offers a cozy, welcoming atmosphere. Visit The Duplex for an authentic and unforgettable night of live entertainment.

8.4 Explore New York City by Night

New York City, famously known as the city that never sleeps, may see a slight decrease in its frenetic pace as evening approaches. However, the Big Apple continues to offer an abundance of exciting activities and experiences well into the night. When planning a trip to this captivating metropolis, it's important to consider not only daytime explorations but also nighttime adventures, regardless of whether you're a morning person or a night owl. The fact is, NYC transforms under the moonlight, revealing a different side to its charm and allure.

To fully experience all that New York City has to offer, here's a list of thrilling activities to enjoy under the serene glow of the moon:

Offer Yourself a Night Walking Tour Experience

New York City buzzes with energy, regardless of whether tourists are present or not. Travelers flock to the Big Apple throughout the year, ensuring that the city's vibrant atmosphere is always on display. One of the best ways to start your vacation is with a daytime walking tour, allowing you to explore the charming streets, marvel at the impressive architecture, and appreciate the diverse mix of people that make up the city's unique spirit.

However, don't overlook the opportunity to embark on a nighttime walking tour, as the contrasting experiences may pleasantly surprise you. While NYC is undeniably beautiful during daylight hours, it takes on an alluring charm when explored after dark. The city's shimmering lights, lively bars, eclectic crowds, enticing restaurants, and other hidden treasures are best experienced at night, making a nocturnal stroll well worth your time.

You can choose to join an organized tour, grab a map and set off on your own adventure, or simply start walking without a specific destination in mind, allowing New York City to reveal its secrets to you. Whichever option you choose, a nighttime walk is undoubtedly one of the most enjoyable activities to experience in Manhattan after the sun goes down.

Indulge in a Late-Night Dinner

Food enthusiasts from around the globe marvel at the diverse culinary experiences offered by the captivating city of New York. With an array of options available to satisfy both locals and visitors' appetites at any time, there is something for everyone.

With so many incredible restaurants to choose from for lunch or early dinner in New York, making a decision can be quite daunting. However, if you've spent the day exploring the city and crave a late-night meal, NYC has plenty of delightful surprises in store for you.

Simply select one of the neighborhoods known for their vibrant nightlife and start exploring until you find a dish that tantalizes your taste buds. The best areas for late-night dining include Midtown, the West Side, and Manhattan's Lower East Side, as well as Brooklyn's Williamsburg.

As for the culinary experiences available in these neighborhoods, the variety is astounding. You'll find everything from sushi and Chinese cuisine to hearty burgers, delectable pizza slices, Latin American dishes, and much more. Whether you prefer street food or a late dinner at a bar open until 11 pm or later, the options are endless.

In conclusion, New York City is a paradise for food lovers from all corners of the world.

A Tranquil Night in Central Park

The remarkable aspect of the renowned Central Park is its ability to provide a peaceful oasis in the midst of a bustling city. However, since many New Yorkers are passionate about sports and outdoor activities, the park itself tends to be quite lively during the day. If you prefer a serene experience and the darkness doesn't intimidate you, strolling around Central Park under the moonlight can be a captivating adventure.

Grab a hot cup of coffee and embark on your walk, paying attention to every corner of the park, as numerous surprises await you. You wouldn't want to miss seeing iconic attractions like the famous Balto and Alice in Wonderland statues!

Enjoy an Evening of Fun: Escape Games in NYC

If you're not traveling solo, you and your friends can have a blast trying to escape from a locked room. Escape games are an intriguing activity because, aside from being entertaining, they also challenge you to think. As you realize you can't figure everything out instantly, you start thinking harder. This activity might be just what you need before unwinding in one of the city's numerous bars.

There are multiple storylines to choose from, with prices typically ranging between $25 to $50 per person. While an escape game isn't cheap, it's definitely worth the investment, especially if you're an adrenaline-seeker.

Experience a Broadway Show

No visitor seeking a complete NYC night experience should miss a Broadway show. Even those on a tight budget should consider this activity, as some fantastic theaters offer discounted tickets. And if you still can't afford a Broadway show, think about off-Broadway and off-off-Broadway performances – not just because they're more affordable, but sometimes they're even better than the most famous ones.

Whether you're traveling with friends, family, or as a solo visitor, watching a Broadway show is undoubtedly an experience that will enhance not only your evening, but your entire trip to the Big Apple.

Enjoy a Friday Night at a Museum

Many visitors don't consider visiting a museum in the evening, but as you might expect, New York is full of delightful surprises for both early birds and night owls. So, don't miss out on spending some memorable moments in places like the Museum of Natural History or the Met when visiting NYC.

These locations, along with other captivating museums, typically stay open late on Fridays. However, when planning your days, make sure to check the schedule on the websites of the spots you want to explore. In addition to extended hours, some museums offer free admission on Fridays. So, if you want to seize such a fantastic deal, think about what you'd like to discover and plan accordingly.

Unwind with Naked Soul or Jazz Music

New Yorkers love listening to live music while savoring their favorite drinks. As a result, the city is brimming with bars where the music is so captivating that you'll want to linger and put your nighttime exploration on hold.

When deciding where to let the amazing music enchant your ears and nourish your soul, keep in mind that many night bars offer special deals. Arrive early, just before 7 pm, and you might catch Happy Hour with its discounted offerings.

You could try the Harlem Jazz Joints (Harlem Jazz Joints out), at around $100 per person, which grants you access to three jazz venues in the Harlem area.

The best Jazz Clubs in Manhattan include:

- Birdland (5402, 315 W 44th St, New York, NY 10036), (212) 581-3080. It opens at 5 PM and closes at midnight. It's a good idea to make a reservation beforehand, and seating is first-come, first-served, so a front-row table isn't guaranteed. Avoid sitting at the bar, as it won't provide an excellent view of the orchestra. Starters here cost around $15, salads around $17, and sandwiches around $18. The venue can accommodate approximately 200 people. There is also a music charge of $25-$50, depending on the performer and seat location. If you attend a Broadway show, you can return with your ticket stub on the same day for half-price bar admission to the 11:00 pm show. Here is a map of the seating in the bar.

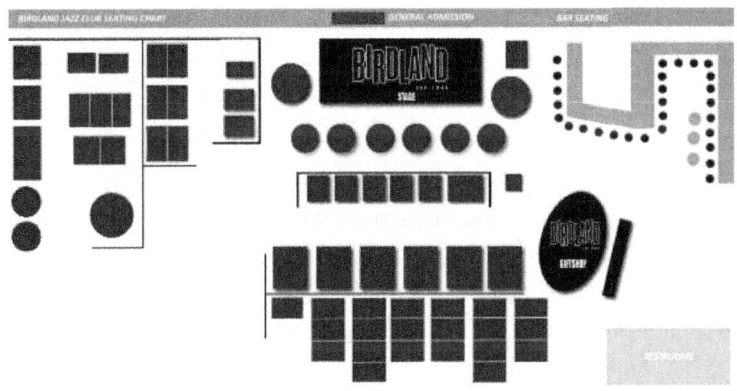

Blue Note (131 W 3rd St, New York, NY 10012): Opening at 6 PM, this legendary jazz bar is most crowded between 9 and 10 PM. While the music is fantastic, the venue can be pricey and packed. Tables are situated shoulder to shoulder, and shows last around 90 minutes before clearing out to accommodate more guests. It's best to make a reservation for either a bar seat (around $30) or a table ($45). Seats are held until 30 minutes before showtime, so arrive no later than 7:30 PM for the first show, 10 PM for the second show, and 12 AM for the Late Night show. Seating is first-come, first-served, so come early for the best seats.

- Smalls Jazz Club (183 W 10th St, New York, NY 10014): This cozy venue features great musicians, long waiting lines, and opens at 7:30 PM. Arrive by 7 PM to secure a spot in line. Admission is $20 per person, and if seated, you'll need to order a drink. The club closes around 4 AM.

- [Village Vanguard](https://www.villagevanguard.com/tickets) (178 7th Ave S, New York, NY 10014, USA): To get excellent seats, make a reservation and arrive 35 minutes before the show. With two performances nightly, the first begins at 8:30 PM (doors open at 7:30) and the second at 10:30 PM (doors open at 10:00 PM). General admission is $35 per set, plus a drink minimum (drinks range from $5 to $16, with a suggested $2-$3 tip per drink). Purchase tickets at https://www.villagevanguard.com/tickets.

- **Jazz Standard** (116 E 27th St, New York, NY 10016): This renowned jazz club is known for its intimate atmosphere and top-notch musical performances. Doors typically open at 6 PM, with shows starting at 7:30 PM and 9:30 PM, and an additional 11:30 PM show on Fridays and Saturdays. It's wise to make a reservation in advance to secure your spot, as the venue can fill up quickly. Tickets range from $20 to $35, depending on the performer, and there's also a $10 food/drink minimum per person. The club shares its space with the acclaimed Blue Smoke restaurant, so you can enjoy delicious barbecue dishes alongside exceptional live jazz. To purchase tickets and check the show schedule, visit their website at https://www.jazzstandard.com/. Remember, seating is first-come, first-served, so arrive early for the best seats.

Admire the Magical Views of the City

NYC is considered by many the ultimate urban beauty. Once you set foot on its charming streets, you will definitely agree with this statement. While exploring its charming neighborhoods is terrific, nothing compares with seeing the city from above, especially by night. Whether you choose to go to the famous Empire State Building, which is open until 2 am, you prefer to go to One World Trade Center Observatory which closes its doors at midnight during summer, or you opt for Top of the Rock (until midnight) your experience will undoubtedly be unforgettable.

People who are extremely afraid of heights usually avoid climbing these three landmarks and just opt for admiring the city lights while walking over the Brooklyn Bridge at night.

Party Like and with the Locals

There are many good reasons why NYC is considered the city that never sleeps and one of them is represented by the fantastic parties available during the whole week. This is why one of the best night activity for people who want to party like a real local is the Pub and Bar Crawls.

Whether you travel by yourself or you are in NYC with your friends a pub crawl is a great idea not only because you get to see the best pubs and bars but also because you have the chance to meet other people and find out interesting things about the nightlife of this fantastic city.

In addition to being a tremendous nighttime activity, the pub crawl is also far from being an expensive one. You will pay between $16-$26 per person and get free entry as well as a couple of drinks. However, if you want more, you will have to pay.

Pampering is Always a Great Idea

Exploring a bustling city like New York can be exhausting, so treating yourself to some relaxation and rejuvenation is not only enjoyable but also essential. The great news is that several top-notch spas in the city stay open late. One local favorite for pampering is Yoga Spa NYC.

If you're yearning for a memorable massage or indulgent spa treatments, don't miss a visit to this luxurious spa. There's no better way to recharge and prepare yourself for another day in the lively New York City.

Embrace Some Touristy Attractions

Many travelers tend to shy away from touristy activities. However, some popular attractions and experiences are genuinely captivating, and it's worth considering them for your itinerary. For example, visiting the Empire State Building is an iconic NYC experience, which is why it holds a special place on many to-do lists. But there are plenty more amazing spots to discover, especially during the evening.

The Rubin Museum houses an impressive collection of Tibetan art, and on Fridays, you can explore the exhibitions until 10 pm while enjoying live music and tasty tapas. This is just one example of the many touristy activities worth experiencing in NYC at night. So, try to avoid skipping things solely because they seem popular among other tourists. Instead, be open to new, thrilling, and spontaneous adventures.

As you can see, the Big Apple has plenty to offer for those who love exploring new places under the gentle moonlight. While it's true that the city's pace slows down somewhat as the night progresses, New York never truly comes to a complete halt. So, plan your nights as carefully as your days in NYC, but remember to stay open to exciting and unexpected experiences.

9. Family-Friendly Activities

9.1 Kid-Friendly Museums and Interactive Exhibits

New York City is home to a wide range of museums and interactive exhibits that cater to children and families. These venues provide engaging, educational experiences that inspire creativity and curiosity, while offering a fun and memorable day out for the whole family. Here are some of the best kid-friendly museums and interactive exhibits in New York City:

1. **American Museum of Natural History**

Website: https://www.amnh.org/ Address: Central Park West & 79th St, New York, NY 10024

The American Museum of Natural History is an iconic institution that offers a vast array of exhibits and displays that will fascinate children of all ages. From the awe-inspiring dinosaur fossils to the breathtaking Hayden Planetarium, this museum is a must-visit destination for families exploring the city.

2. **Children's Museum of Manhattan**

Website: https://cmom.org/ Address: 212 W 83rd St, New York, NY 10024

The Children's Museum of Manhattan is specifically designed for children aged 0-10, offering five floors of interactive exhibits, hands-on activities, and creative workshops. The museum's exhibits focus on art, science, and culture, providing an enriching and entertaining experience for young visitors.

3. **New York Hall of Science**

Website: https://nysci.org/ Address: 47-01 111th St, Queens, NY 11368

Located in Queens, the New York Hall of Science is an interactive science center that offers more than 450 hands-on exhibits, workshops, and demonstrations. With a focus on STEM subjects, the museum encourages learning through play and exploration, making it an ideal destination for curious young minds.

4. **Intrepid Sea, Air & Space Museum**

Website: https://www.intrepidmuseum.org/ Address: Pier 86, W 46th St & 12th Ave, New York, NY 10036

The Intrepid Sea, Air & Space Museum, housed on the historic aircraft carrier Intrepid, offers an immersive experience that transports visitors through history, science, and technology. With a range of aircraft, submarines, and space vehicles on display, this museum is sure to captivate children interested in transportation and exploration.

5. **Brooklyn Children's Museum**

Website: https://www.brooklynkids.org/ Address: 145 Brooklyn Ave, Brooklyn, NY 11213

The Brooklyn Children's Museum, founded in 1899, was the first museum created specifically for children. With interactive exhibits focusing on art, culture, and the environment, this museum offers a range of experiences that are both educational and engaging for young visitors.

6. **The Strong National Museum of Play**

Website: https://www.museumofplay.org/ Address: One Manhattan Square, Rochester, NY 14607

Located in nearby Rochester, The Strong National Museum of Play is a family-friendly destination dedicated to the history and exploration of play. The museum features a variety of interactive exhibits, including the popular Toy Halls of Fame, the World Video Game Hall of Fame, and hands-on displays for children of all ages.

9.2 Urban Adventures: Zoos, Aquariums, and Amusement Parks

New York City and its surrounding areas offer a wealth of urban adventures for families and thrill-seekers alike. From world-class zoos and aquariums to iconic amusement parks, these attractions provide a unique and memorable experience for visitors of all ages. Here are some of the top zoos, aquariums, and amusement parks to explore during your visit to New York City:

1. **Bronx Zoo**

Website: https://bronxzoo.com/ Address: 2300 Southern Blvd, Bronx, NY 10460

The Bronx Zoo, located in the borough of the Bronx, is the largest urban zoo in the United States, spanning 265 acres and featuring more than 6,000 animals. With its diverse range of habitats and species, the zoo offers an immersive and educational experience for visitors, who can observe animals from around the world, including lions, tigers, gorillas, and more.

2. **New York Aquarium**

Website: https://nyaquarium.com/ Address: 602 Surf Ave, Brooklyn, NY 11224

Situated on Coney Island in Brooklyn, the New York Aquarium is home to a wide variety of marine life, including sea lions, sharks, and penguins. With engaging exhibits like the Ocean Wonders: Sharks! and the Aquatheater, this attraction provides an unforgettable experience for visitors interested in exploring the wonders of the underwater world.

3. **Central Park Zoo**

Website: https://centralparkzoo.com/ Address: E 64th St & 5th Ave, New York, NY 10021

Located in the heart of Manhattan, the Central Park Zoo is a charming, compact zoo that offers an intimate and engaging experience for visitors. With a range of exhibits featuring animals such as snow leopards, sea lions, and red pandas, this urban oasis provides a delightful escape from the hustle and bustle of the city.

4. **Coney Island's Luna Park**

Website: https://lunaparknyc.com/ Address: 1000 Surf Ave, Brooklyn, NY 11224

Luna Park, located on Coney Island in Brooklyn, is a historic amusement park that has been entertaining visitors since 1903. With its iconic rides, such as the Cyclone roller coaster and the Wonder Wheel, Luna Park offers a nostalgic and thrilling experience for the whole family. Don't forget to try the famous Nathan's Famous hot dogs while you're there!

5. **Victorian Gardens Amusement Park**

Website: https://victoriangardensnyc.com/ Address: Wollman Rink, Central Park, New York, NY 10019

Nestled within Central Park, Victorian Gardens Amusement Park is a seasonal attraction that offers a charming, family-friendly experience. With its traditional, carnival-style rides and games, this small-scale amusement park provides an enchanting and delightful day out for younger children.

6. **Adventureland**

Website: https://adventureland.us/ Address: 2245 Broadhollow Rd, Farmingdale, NY 11735

Located on Long Island, Adventureland is a family-friendly amusement park that offers a variety of rides and attractions for visitors of all ages. With roller coasters, water rides, and an arcade, this park provides a fun and exciting day out for the whole family.

9.3 Educational and Fun Workshops for the Whole Family

New York City offers numerous workshops that cater to families, providing educational and entertaining experiences for all ages. These workshops range from hands-on art and science programs to cooking classes and storytelling sessions. Here are some of the best family-friendly workshops in New York City, where you can learn, create, and bond together:

1. **Brooklyn Robot Foundry**

At the Brooklyn Robot Foundry, families can explore the world of robotics through hands-on workshops and classes. Participants learn about engineering concepts, problem-solving, and collaboration while building their own robots using various materials and tools. This creative and interactive environment is perfect for both kids and adults.

Website: https://brooklynrobotfoundry.com/ Address: 1595 2nd Ave, New York, NY 10028

2. **Taste Buds Kitchen**

Taste Buds Kitchen offers a variety of cooking workshops for families, where participants can learn to prepare delicious dishes from around the world. These interactive classes are designed for kids and adults, with the goal of fostering a love for cooking and promoting healthy eating habits.

Website: https://tastebudskitchen.com/nyc/ Address: 109 W 27th St, New York, NY 10001

3. **The Art Studio NY**

The Art Studio NY provides a welcoming and nurturing environment for families to explore their artistic talents. Their family art workshops cater to all skill levels, with experienced instructors guiding participants through various techniques and mediums, such as painting, drawing, and sculpture.

Website: https://www.theartstudiony.com/ Address: 145 W 96th St, New York, NY 10025

4. **The Story Pirates**

The Story Pirates offer interactive storytelling workshops that inspire creativity and imagination in children and their families. These workshops combine theater, comedy, and music, providing a unique and engaging experience that promotes literacy and encourages self-expression.

Website: https://www.storypirates.com/ Address: Various locations throughout NYC

5. New York Botanical Garden

The New York Botanical Garden hosts a variety of family workshops, where participants can learn about plants, flowers, and gardening. These hands-on programs explore topics such as plant science, art, and nature, providing an enriching and educational experience for the whole family.

Website: https://www.nybg.org/ Address: 2900 Southern Blvd, Bronx, NY 10458

6. Textile Arts Center

The Textile Arts Center offers a range of family-friendly workshops that focus on various textile techniques, such as weaving, sewing, and embroidery. Participants learn traditional skills while creating their own unique projects, fostering creativity and self-expression in a supportive and collaborative environment.

Website: https://www.textileartscenter.com/ Address: 505 Carroll St, Brooklyn, NY 11215

These family-friendly workshops in New York City provide a perfect opportunity for families to bond, learn, and have fun together while exploring new interests and developing new skills.

10. Seasonal Events and Festivals

10.1 Winter Wonderland: Ice Skating, Holiday Markets, and Festive Lights

New York City transforms into a magical winter wonderland during the colder months, offering a variety of festive activities and attractions for visitors to enjoy. From ice skating rinks and holiday markets to dazzling light displays, the city provides a memorable and enchanting experience for all ages. Here are some of the best winter activities to enjoy in New York City:

1. **Ice Skating Rinks** New York City boasts several iconic ice skating rinks that offer a quintessential winter experience. The Rink at Rockefeller Center, located beneath the famous Christmas tree, is a popular destination for tourists and locals alike. Other notable rinks include Wollman Rink in Central Park, Bryant Park's Winter Village, and Brookfield Place's rink in Lower Manhattan. Various locations throughout NYC

2. **Holiday Markets** The city's holiday markets are perfect for those seeking unique and festive gifts. These seasonal markets offer a wide range of artisanal products, from handmade jewelry and crafts to gourmet food items. Some popular holiday markets include the Union Square Holiday Market, the Columbus Circle Holiday Market, and the Winter Village at Bryant Park. Various locations throughout NYC

3. **Festive Lights and Decorations** New York City comes alive with dazzling light displays and decorations during the holiday season. The Dyker Heights neighborhood in Brooklyn is famous for its extravagant light displays, attracting visitors from all over the world. Other must-see attractions include the holiday window displays along Fifth Avenue, the Christmas tree at Rockefeller Center, and the light show at Saks Fifth Avenue. Various locations throughout NYC

4. **Holiday Shows and Performances** The city offers a variety of festive shows and performances throughout the winter season. The Radio City

Christmas Spectacular, featuring the world-famous Rockettes, is a beloved holiday tradition. Other popular shows include George Balanchine's The Nutcracker at the New York City Ballet, and A Christmas Carol at the Theatre at St. Clement's. Various locations throughout NYC

5. **New Year's Eve in Times Square** No visit to New York City during the holiday season would be complete without experiencing the iconic New Year's Eve celebration in Times Square. This world-famous event features live performances, confetti, and the thrilling countdown to the New Year, culminating in the ball drop at midnight. Location: Times Square, New York, NY

With its enchanting winter activities and attractions, New York City offers a truly magical experience during the holiday season, creating lasting memories for visitors and residents alike.

10.2 Spring Blossoms: Cherry Blossoms, Macy's Flower Show, and Easter Parade

As winter fades, New York City comes alive with the vibrant colors and fragrances of spring. From cherry blossoms and flower shows to festive parades, the city offers a range of activities and events that celebrate the season's renewal. Here are some of the top spring attractions in New York City:

1. **Cherry Blossoms**

New York City is home to several parks and gardens where visitors can admire the delicate beauty of cherry blossoms. The Brooklyn Botanic Garden hosts the annual Sakura Matsuri Cherry Blossom Festival, a weekend-long celebration of Japanese culture and the blossoming cherry trees. Other notable cherry blossom viewing spots include Central Park, Riverside Park, and Randall's Island Park. Various locations throughout NYC

2. **Macy's Flower Show**

The Macy's Flower Show is a beloved annual event that takes place at the iconic Macy's Herald Square. This two-week-long exhibition features stunning floral displays, themed gardens, and special events. Visitors can marvel at the elaborate arrangements created by skilled florists, and even participate in workshops and demonstrations.

Location: Macy's Herald Square, 151 W 34th St, New York, NY 10001

3. **Easter Parade and Bonnet Festival**

The Easter Parade and Bonnet Festival is a quirky and colorful New York City tradition. Held annually on Easter Sunday, this festive procession showcases a wide array of whimsical and creative bonnets. Participants stroll along Fifth Avenue, from St. Patrick's Cathedral to 57th Street, providing a delightful and entertaining spectacle for all ages.

Location: Fifth Avenue, from St. Patrick's Cathedral to 57th Street, New York, NY

4. **Daffodil Project and Tulip Festival**

The Daffodil Project, a citywide beautification initiative, fills New York City's parks, gardens, and public spaces with vibrant daffodils each spring. In addition, the annual Tulip Festival at the West Side Community Garden showcases thousands of tulips in a stunning array of colors. These floral displays provide a perfect backdrop for leisurely strolls and picnics in the park.

5. **Earth Day Celebrations**

New York City hosts numerous events and activities in honor of Earth Day each April. These celebrations promote environmental awareness and sustainable practices, with events such as educational workshops, eco-friendly product exhibitions, and tree-planting initiatives. The annual Earth Day New York event takes place in Union Square, featuring live performances, interactive displays, and activities for all ages. Location: Union Square, New York, NY

Embrace the beauty and vitality of spring in New York City by partaking in these seasonal events and attractions. From blossoming flowers to festive parades, the city offers a lively and rejuvenating experience for visitors and residents alike.

10.3 Summer in the City: Outdoor Movies, Concerts, and Street Fairs

Summertime in New York City is marked by long, sunny days and a vibrant atmosphere. The city comes alive with an array of outdoor events, offering residents and visitors the chance to enjoy movies, concerts, and street fairs beneath the open sky. Here are some of the most popular summer activities in the city:

1. **Outdoor Movies**

New York City hosts numerous outdoor movie screenings in parks and public spaces during the summer months. These events offer a unique and relaxed movie-watching experience under the stars. Some popular venues include the Bryant Park Movie Nights, Rooftop Films at various locations, and Movies with a View at Brooklyn Bridge Park.

2. **Summer Concerts**

Free outdoor concerts are a staple of the New York City summer experience. From classical music to contemporary pop, there's something for everyone. Some noteworthy concert series include Central Park's SummerStage, the BRIC Celebrate Brooklyn! Festival at Prospect Park, and Lincoln Center Out of Doors. Additionally, many parks host local musicians and bands throughout the summer.

3. **Street Fairs and Festivals**

Street fairs and festivals are a great way to explore New York City's diverse neighborhoods, sample delicious food, and discover unique crafts and goods. These events typically feature live music, art exhibitions, and family-friendly activities. Some popular events include the Ninth Avenue International Food Festival, the Hester Street Fair, and the Smorgasburg food market in Brooklyn.

4. **Outdoor Theater and Performances**

New York City's parks and public spaces become stages for outdoor theater and performances during the summer months. The most famous of these is the Public Theater's Shakespeare in the Park, which offers free productions of the bard's works at the Delacorte Theater in Central Park. Other outdoor theater options include the New York Classical Theatre and the Summer Theatre Festival at the Flea Theater

5. **Beaches and Pools**

When the temperatures rise, New Yorkers flock to the city's beaches and public pools to cool off. Coney Island, Rockaway Beach, and Orchard Beach are among the most popular seaside destinations. The city also offers numerous public pools, including the Astoria Park Pool, McCarren Park Pool, and the Lasker Pool in Central Park.

Summer in New York City is a time of fun and excitement, with countless outdoor events and activities to suit every taste. From open-air movies and concerts to street fairs and beaches, there's no shortage of ways to enjoy the city's warm and lively atmosphere.

10.4 Fall Foliage: Halloween Celebrations and Thanksgiving Traditions

As the leaves begin to change and the air turns crisp, New York City embraces the beauty of autumn with a host of seasonal events and traditions. From Halloween festivities to Thanksgiving celebrations, the city offers a range of activities for visitors and residents to enjoy during this picturesque time of year. Here are some of the highlights of autumn in New York City:

1. **Fall Foliage**

New York City's parks and gardens become a tapestry of vibrant colors during the fall, providing the perfect backdrop for leisurely strolls and photo opportunities. Central Park, Prospect Park, and the New York Botanical Garden are among the top spots for admiring the changing leaves. For an elevated view, head to the Top of the Rock or the Empire State Building's observation deck. Various locations throughout NYC

2. Halloween Celebrations

The city comes alive with spooky and creative Halloween festivities throughout October. The annual Village Halloween Parade is a must-see event, featuring a dazzling display of costumes, music, and dancing. Other popular Halloween events include the Great Jack O'Lantern Blaze, the Tompkins Square Park Halloween Dog Parade, and the Boo at the Zoo event at the Bronx Zoo. Various locations throughout NYC

3. Thanksgiving Traditions

Thanksgiving in New York City is a time for family, friends, and festive events. The Macy's Thanksgiving Day Parade is an iconic celebration featuring giant balloons, elaborate floats, and live performances. Other Thanksgiving activities include the Turkey Trot races in various parks and the traditional lighting of the Christmas tree at Rockefeller Center, marking the start of the holiday season. Various locations throughout NYC

4. Fall Harvest Festivals

Celebrate the bounty of the season at one of New York City's many fall harvest festivals. These events often include pumpkin patches, hayrides, apple picking, and other autumn-themed activities. Some notable events include the Queens County Farm Museum's Fall Harvest Festival, the New York Botanical Garden's Harvest Homecoming, and the Greenbelt Conservancy's Pumpkin Festival. Various locations throughout NYC

5. Fall Food and Drink Events

New York City's culinary scene embraces the flavors of fall with a variety of food and drink events. From Oktoberfest celebrations featuring German beer and cuisine to food festivals highlighting seasonal ingredients, there's something for every palate. Don't miss the New York City Wine & Food Festival, the Big Apple Crunch, and the New York Oyster Week. Various locations throughout NYC

Autumn in New York City offers a vibrant and enchanting experience, with its stunning fall foliage, festive events, and beloved traditions. Whether you're visiting for the first time or a lifelong resident, there's no shortage of ways to enjoy the city during this magical time of year.

11. Practical Information

11.1 Accommodation: Hotels, Hostels, and Vacation Rentals

Finding the perfect place to stay is a crucial part of any trip to New York City. The city offers a wide range of accommodation options, catering to different preferences, budgets, and travel styles. Whether you're looking for luxury hotels, budget-friendly hostels, or the comforts of a vacation rental, New York City has something for everyone. Here are some of the top accommodation options in the city:

1. **Hotels**

New York City is home to some of the world's most famous and luxurious hotels, such as The Plaza, The Ritz-Carlton, and The St. Regis. These upscale establishments offer lavish amenities, top-notch service, and prime locations. However, the city also has a variety of mid-range and budget hotels, like the Pod Hotels or citizenM, that provide comfortable and affordable stays without compromising on quality.

2. **Hostels**

For travelers on a budget or looking for a social atmosphere, hostels are an excellent choice. New York City has a wide selection of hostels offering dormitory-style rooms, private rooms, and shared facilities. Some popular options include HI NYC Hostel, The Local, and Freehand New York. Many hostels also organize events and activities, making it easy to meet fellow travelers.

3. **Vacation Rentals**

Vacation rentals, such as Airbnb or Vrbo, are a popular choice for visitors seeking the comforts of home while exploring the city. These options provide the opportunity to stay in residential neighborhoods and experience life as a local. Vacation rentals range from shared rooms and private apartments to entire houses, catering to various group sizes and budgets.

4. **Boutique Hotels**

Boutique hotels offer a unique and personalized experience, often featuring stylish interiors, attentive service, and a distinct character. Some noteworthy boutique hotels in New York City include The NoMad Hotel, The Bowery Hotel, and The High Line Hotel. These properties provide a more intimate and luxurious alternative to larger chain hotels.

5. **Bed and Breakfasts**

Bed and breakfasts are a charming and cozy option for those seeking a more intimate and personal lodging experience. These establishments typically offer a small number of rooms, a friendly atmosphere, and a home-cooked breakfast each morning. Some popular bed and breakfasts in New York City include The Harbor House, The Urban Cowboy, and The Lafayette House.

11.2 Where to Stay in NYC: Exploring Manhattan's Vibrant Districts

New York City, with its ten million inhabitants, is made up of five main areas, including the iconic Manhattan, home to over three million people. Manhattan epitomizes New York City with its towering skyscrapers, bustling Central Park, abundant shopping, dining, and yellow taxis.

Manhattan's Districts: Manhattan is an island nestled between two rivers, comprising several vibrant districts such as Midtown, SoHo, East Village, Meatpacking District, NoLIta, Financial District, Greenwich Village, Little Italy, Chinatown, Upper East Side, and Harlem.

- **Midtown**: The most central area in Manhattan, Midtown is situated between Times Square and the Empire State Building or between Fifth and Seventh Avenue around Times Square. This bustling district is home to iconic attractions and a plethora of accommodations, making it an ideal base for exploring the city. However, keep in mind that the area can be noisy and crowded, which might not suit everyone.
- **SoHo**: Known for its chic shopping, luxury brands, and numerous cafes, bars, and restaurants, SoHo offers a more upscale and fashionable

experience. This area is perfect for visitors seeking a stylish and trendy neighborhood with a vibrant atmosphere.
- **Chinatown**: Boasting the highest density of Chinese residents outside of China, Chinatown offers an authentic and immersive cultural experience. Here, you'll find an array of Asian markets, eateries, and shops. Staying in Chinatown is ideal for those interested in experiencing the rich cultural diversity of New York City.
- **Meatpacking District**: Renowned for its vibrant nightlife, the Meatpacking District is home to numerous bars, clubs, and the famous Chelsea Market. This area is perfect for travelers seeking a lively and energetic atmosphere, with plenty of entertainment options.
- **East Village**: Featuring a more relaxed, bohemian vibe, East Village is teeming with restaurants, cafes, and independent shops. This neighborhood is ideal for visitors who prefer a laid-back, artistic atmosphere with a strong sense of community.

When selecting your accommodation in Manhattan, consider that staying outside of the island may result in longer travel times to popular attractions. While Manhattan is generally more expensive, it's important to factor in potential costs such as taxes, breakfast, and Wi-Fi when comparing options. Budget-conscious travelers may want to look for alternatives, such as hostels or Airbnb, but should be aware that even these options can be pricey in New York City.

The best area to stay in Manhattan is arguably between Fifth and Seventh Avenue, below Times Square. However, Manhattan's excellent subway system makes it easy to reach popular areas regardless of your lodging choice. It's advisable to avoid staying in Harlem, north of Central Park, as it offers limited attractions and requires additional travel time to reach downtown.

1 The Club Quarters Downtown is our Suggested Hotel in NYC

One of our top recommended hotels in NYC is Club Quarters Downtown, located at 52 Williams Street, New York, NY 10005. You can reach them by phone at (212) 269-6400. This hotel offers clean rooms, exceptional staff, and stunning views. It's conveniently situated near the Financial District, Staten Island Ferry, and various public transportation options. To read reviews and check prices, click here (rated 8.1/10). While not centrally located, being in the Financial District at the southern end of Manhattan, you can easily access all the sights using the nearby subway. The price for a night's stay in a room with one bed for two people is $189/night.

[Club Quarters Downtown, click here to Read the Reviews and Check the Prices](#)

Insight About This Hotel: Fantastic location. We stayed at this hotel for several nights and found the location, just off Wall Street, to be ideal. A short 10-minute walk took us to the waterfront with stunning views of Brooklyn and the Bridge. The subway station was only a minute away, making it convenient to explore the city. The rooms were clean and featured free Wi-Fi, a wonderful perk. Just a 5-minute walk away, we discovered the lively bars of Stone Street, nestled along a charming cobbled street. The vibrant atmosphere here is a must-experience, especially during happy hour. Check-in and check-out processes were quick and hassle-free.

We also recommend considering the Holiday Inn Express Times Square South ($170) and The Standard Hotel at High Line ($300).

Holiday Inn Express Times Square South is situated in an excellent location, right in the heart of Manhattan. It offers free breakfast, which, while not exceptional, will keep you satisfied for a few hours. Complimentary Wi-Fi, clean rooms, and a luggage room where you can store your belongings if your flight departs later in the day make it a great value for your money, particularly if you can book a room for under $190 per night. We stayed at this hotel for eight nights and can confidently recommend it, especially if you find a rate between $170 and $190. The free breakfast includes pancakes, bananas, apples, Greek yogurt, omelets, sausages (which may not be to everyone's taste), coffee, tea, honey, and a few other items. Free water is also provided, and you can fill up your bottles at no extra charge, potentially saving you a significant amount since a small 500ml bottle of water in NYC costs $2.75.

- [Holiday Inn Express Times Square South](#)

- [Standard hotel](#)

[The Standard Hotel at the Highline](#) is more costly, but it boasts a stunning interior design and is located in the heart of the Meatpacking District. Additionally, the hotel houses one of NYC's most renowned clubs, "Le Bain," and features an incredible bar on the 18th floor, offering some of the best views in the city. A nearby subway station makes it easy to travel to other popular destinations. The Standard Hotel is situated at the beginning of the famous High Line, a park built atop old railway tracks.

Cheap Options for Your Stay in NYC

We recommend the following options if you have a strict budget; however, if possible, consider making additional room in your budget for a better accommodation experience.

Under $100:

- Village Apartments in Greenwich Village is a decent, budget-friendly choice. This complex of apartments offers basic amenities and is located at 11 Waverly Place.
- Chelsea Inn, situated at 46 W 17th St between 5th and 6th Ave, is another affordable option (http://www.chelseainn.com/). Rates start at $89 per night.

Alternatively, explore accommodations on Homeaway.com or Airbnb.com. If you're traveling solo, consider booking a shared room to save even more money.

11.2 Staying Connected: Wi-Fi, Cell Phones, and Internet Cafes

In today's digital age, staying connected while traveling is essential. Whether you're keeping in touch with loved ones, updating social media, or working remotely, having access to Wi-Fi, cell phone service, and internet cafes is crucial. Here's a guide to help you stay connected while exploring New York City and Manhattan.

Wi-Fi:

1. Public Wi-Fi: New York City offers free public Wi-Fi in many areas, including parks, public libraries, and subway stations. The city's largest public Wi-Fi network, LinkNYC, provides free, fast Wi-Fi through kiosks called Links. They also offer USB charging ports, phone calls, and access to city services.

2. Hotels and accommodations: Most hotels, hostels, and vacation rentals provide Wi-Fi access, either free or for a fee. Confirm Wi-Fi availability and any additional costs when booking your accommodation.

3. Cafes and restaurants: Many cafes and restaurants in New York City offer free Wi-Fi to their customers. Starbucks, Pret A Manger, and McDonald's are among the popular chains with free Wi-Fi. Local coffee shops and eateries may also provide Wi-Fi access.

Cell Phones:

1. International roaming: Check with your cell phone provider for international roaming options and associated costs. Some carriers offer affordable roaming packages or daily passes for travelers.

2. Local SIM card: If you have an unlocked phone, consider purchasing a local SIM card upon arrival in New York City. This can be a cost-effective way to stay connected, with options for data, text, and voice plans from carriers like AT&T, T-Mobile, and Verizon.

3. Rental phones: Some companies offer rental phones for travelers, which can be a convenient option if you don't have an unlocked phone or don't want to use your own device.

Internet Cafes:

While internet cafes are less common in New York City due to widespread Wi-Fi availability, there are still some locations where you can find computers with internet access. These establishments usually charge a fee for usage by the minute or hour. Some internet cafes may also offer additional services like printing, scanning, and faxing.

By following this guide, you can ensure that you stay connected while enjoying your time in New York City and Manhattan.

11.3 Health and Safety: Travel Insurance, Hospitals, and Emergency Contacts

When visiting New York City and Manhattan, it's essential to prioritize your health and safety. Having the right travel insurance, knowing the locations of hospitals, and having emergency contacts on hand will help you feel prepared and protected during your trip.

Travel Insurance:

Purchasing travel insurance before your trip is a smart decision. It can cover various expenses such as medical emergencies, trip cancellations, lost luggage, and more. Compare policies and choose one that suits your needs and budget. Be sure to read the fine print and understand what's covered and what's not before committing to a policy.

Hospitals:

New York City has numerous hospitals and medical facilities, many of which provide world-class care. In case of emergencies, it's essential to know the nearest hospital to your accommodation. Some of the major hospitals in Manhattan include:

1. NewYork-Presbyterian Hospital (525 E 68th St, New York, NY 10065)
2. Mount Sinai Hospital (1468 Madison Ave, New York, NY 10029)
3. NYU Langone Health (550 1st Avenue, New York, NY 10016)
4. Bellevue Hospital Center (462 1st Avenue, New York, NY 10016)

Keep in mind that walk-in clinics and urgent care centers are also available for non-emergency medical issues. These facilities can often provide faster service and are more affordable than emergency rooms.

Emergency Contacts:

In case of emergencies, it's crucial to have important phone numbers readily available. Here are some essential contacts to have on hand during your trip to New York City:

1. Emergency Services (Police, Fire, Ambulance): Dial 911
2. Non-Emergency Police: Dial 311
3. New York City Poison Control Center: (212) 764-7667 or (800) 222-1222
4. U.S. Embassy and Consulates: Look up the contact information for your country's embassy or consulate in New York City. This can be helpful in case of lost passports, legal issues, or other emergencies.

Additionally, consider sharing your travel itinerary with a friend or family member, so someone knows your whereabouts and can be contacted in case of emergencies.

By taking these health and safety precautions, you can ensure a more enjoyable and worry-free trip to New York City and Manhattan.

11.4 Best Tips and Recommendations for your travel to NYC

To make your trip to NYC more enjoyable and hassle-free, keep these helpful tips in mind before you arrive:

- Print your ESTA documents and have the address of your accommodation ready, as you'll need to provide this information upon arrival.

- Bring a pen to fill out any required documents handed to you during your flight.

- Pre-book your Broadway theater show tickets online to secure your seats.

- Request an upper floor room when booking your hotel if you're sensitive to noise, but be prepared for potentially longer elevator wait times.

- Be aware that many places, such as cafes and bars, do not offer free Wi-Fi.

- New Yorkers can be incredibly friendly but may also be blunt or impatient. Be prepared for a mix of attitudes.

- NYC is a very LGBTQ+ friendly city. Embrace the openness and be respectful of others.

- Some hotels charge for Wi-Fi access and do not offer free breakfast.

- Restrooms in many places require a code for entry, which can be found on your receipt or by asking employees. Restrooms are often unisex.
- Make restaurant reservations in advance using the OpenTable app or by visiting the restaurant's website.
- Find free Wi-Fi spots by visiting: https://www.nycgo.com/articles/wifi-in-nyc

Download these useful apps on your mobile phone:

- TodayTix for discounted Broadway show tickets
- Discotech for guest list access to clubs
- MoMA Audio for a guide to the Museum of Modern Art
- Google Arts & Culture for art-related content
- Yelp for finding happy hour menus and saving money
- Eat St. for tracking food trucks and their daily locations
- OpenTable for restaurant reservations
- NYC Subway for navigating the subway system
- Shake Shack for pre-ordering from the popular burger chain to avoid waiting in line
- Download the offline Google Map of Manhattan to avoid mobile data charges while navigating the city.
- Obtain a MetroCard (MTA): The price for a one-week unlimited MTA MetroCard is $33. You can purchase it at various locations, including Grand Central Terminal, and it can be paid for with a credit card. This MetroCard provides you with unlimited access to both the subway system and buses in New York City. Without an unlimited card, a single ride on the subway costs $2.50.

- Water Tip: Buying water in NYC can be expensive, with a small bottle costing around $2.70. A more cost-effective solution is to visit a local supermarket and purchase multiple larger bottles of water. For example, a 1.5-liter bottle of water typically costs around $1.60 at a supermarket. Popular chains include Whole Foods and Trader Joe's. Use Google Maps to find the nearest location to you.

- Free wifi spots: https://www.nycgo.com/articles/wifi-in-nyc

Navigating NYC Roads:

• Manhattan's layout is simple to understand once you grasp the basic concepts, such as the distinction between streets and avenues and the progression of their numbers. In Manhattan, there are both streets and avenues.

• Avenues run vertically (north to south) and begin in the east with First Avenue. Fifth Avenue is the central vertical road of Manhattan, while Eleventh Avenue is the last.

• Streets run horizontally (east to west) and start in the south with First Street. As you move north, the street numbers increase. For example, Central Park is located at 59th Street.

• When walking along the south-north axis, 20 blocks equal a mile. For instance, walking north on Fifth Avenue from 40th Street to 60th Street is a mile. This translates to about a 1-minute walk per street or 20 minutes per mile.

• The distance between avenues varies, but it generally takes around 3 minutes to walk from one avenue to the next.

Nightlife: Le Bain

Le Bain, located at the Standard Hotel on the HighLine, is one of the most popular clubbing spots in Manhattan. Entry to Le Bain is on the ground floor and is free if you can pass the door control. Admission criteria can be seemingly random, and it's not solely based on appearance or attire. If you're not granted access, they may claim the party is invitation-only. However, you can still visit the 18th-floor lounge bar, which offers stunning views, excellent cocktails ($20), and no door policy. Just remember to leave your coats in the cloakroom.

Tip: Make sure to use the restroom while you're there; we won't spoil the surprise by telling you why.

Nightlife: Apollo Theater, Harlem

Every Wednesday, the Apollo Theater hosts Amateur Nights, an exciting event where up-and-coming talents perform on stage with the hopes of making it big. These nights are a fantastic opportunity to witness potential future stars in action. To attend, you can purchase tickets online through the Apollo Theater's website.

Money-Saving Tip: MoMA Free Nights on Fridays (4:00 to 8 pm):

Gain free admission for all visitors during UNIQLO Free Friday Nights, held every Friday evening from 4:00 to 8:00 p.m. To sidestep lengthy queues, it's best to arrive after 6:00 p.m. and avoid bringing oversized bags, as anything larger than 11 × 15 × 5" must be checked. The line for UNIQLO Free Friday tickets starts at the Museum's 54th Street entrance. Your ticket allows access to all galleries and exhibitions. However, large crowds can make it challenging to appreciate the art peacefully. For instance, you'll likely encounter numerous people trying to snap a photo of Van Gogh's Starry Night painting. Free Fridays may not be suitable for those who dislike crowded spaces.

Keep in mind that there is another art museum, the Metropolitan Museum of Art, which is entirely separate from MoMA. Don't confuse the two!

Two helpful tips for visiting MoMA: first, download the MoMA audio app before your visit; second, download the Google Arts & Culture app and search for MoMA exhibits.

Chelsea Market: A Must-Visit Food Destination in NYC

Chelsea Market is NYC's most popular food market and well worth a visit. Begin your journey at Hudson Yards and make your way to the High Line, a park built atop old train rails. At some point, descend from the High Line to enter Chelsea Market, a covered market offering food and clothing in an industrial-style setting that boasts a unique charm.

Stop by the Lobster Place and order the Lobster Roll ($21). You'll have to wait for 10 to 15 minutes at the back window with a number in hand, and the sandwich may not be large, but it's certainly fresh and delicious. There's no seating inside the Lobster Place, so you'll have to eat standing up or grab a table in the main lobby of Chelsea Market.

The market also features numerous other shops offering sushi, steaks, French, Italian, and Mexican cuisine, or you can head one level down and create your own salad.

After leaving Chelsea Market, walk about a kilometer to reach the iconic Carrie Bradshaw apartment from the Sex and the City show in Greenwich Village. You can find it on Google Maps, and when you arrive, you'll likely see a chain in front of the steps and people snapping photos.

NBA Tickets

Catch an NBA game at the world-renowned Madison Square Garden, home of the New York Knicks, on Saturdays at 7:30 pm. Purchase tickets online, with the cheapest seats starting at $69 per person.

Brooklyn Bridge

For comprehensive information on the Brooklyn Bridge, visit https://freetoursbyfoot.com/walking-the-brooklyn-bridge/. Begin on the Brooklyn side and walk towards Manhattan for the best views. Take the subway to Jay Street station in Manhattan. Tip 1: Find discounted Broadway tickets at the TKTS sales shop outside the Jay Street subway station. Tip 2: Grab a burrito ($12) or tacos ($11) at the nearby Chipotle Mexican Grill. The 2km bridge walk takes around 40 minutes, considering stops for photos. The walkway is divided into sections for bikes and pedestrians.

NYC Observation Decks

Manhattan has three observation decks: the Empire State Building, Top of the Rock, and One World Trade Center. Admission to each is around $30 to $35 per person. First-timers typically visit the Empire State Building, while Top of the Rock offers timed entry and panoramic views.

Top Coffee Spots

Visit Joe and the Juice, Balthazar, and O Cafe in Little Italy, as well as Laduree in Soho, Two Hands Cafe in Little Italy, Epistrophy in Little Italy, Think Coffee in Noho, and Eataly at Madison Square.

Outlets

Check out one of the Century 21 stores in Manhattan for discounted shopping, with the largest store located near the World Trade Center. For an even bigger selection, visit Woodbury Outlets, 80km away, with bus transportation available for $40 to $50 per person.

Broadway Shows

The Phantom of the Opera at the Majestic Theater near Times Square is a classic choice. Purchase tickets online, and don't forget to print them. No need to overdress or arrive too early, as entry is quick. The Majestic Theater is vast, so cheaper seats offer a limited view. Food and drink are available for purchase inside, and no phones or photos are allowed during the performance.

TKTS Broadway Sales

Find discounted same-day Broadway tickets at TKTS shops around Manhattan. Best time to arrive is around 5 pm when all available tickets are released. Expect to wait in line for 30 to 60 minutes.

About the Subway

Although the subway system in NYC is old, sometimes dirty, and smelly, it has been in operation for over a century. Generally, only about thirty steps separate the ground level from the subway. Most lines run north to south, while buses cover east to west routes. The subway is mostly safe, and using common sense should keep you out of trouble. Opting for a Metrocard with unlimited access for several days can save money, time, and energy.

Central Park

Located just outside Central Park at 72nd Street is the Dakota Building, a cooperative built in 1890. It was home to John Lennon and the site of his tragic murder. Yoko Ono still resides there. Bike rentals are available for around $15 for three hours, and you can also rent boats on the park's lake.

Suggested First-Day Walking Tour in Manhattan:

If you prefer to skip visiting the Statue of Liberty and want to explore the heart of Manhattan on your first day in the city, we suggest the following walking tour itinerary:

1. Start at Grand Central Terminal: Begin your journey at the iconic Grand Central Terminal, which is not only a transportation hub but also an architectural marvel. Take time to appreciate the stunning main concourse with its constellation ceiling and the grand marble staircases.

2. Head to the Chrysler Building: A short walk from Grand Central, the Chrysler Building is an Art Deco masterpiece that once held the title of the world's tallest building. While its interior is not open to the public, the exterior is still worth admiring.

3. Visit the New York Public Library: Continue your walk to the New York Public Library's Stephen A. Schwarzman Building. Explore its majestic Rose Main Reading Room on the third floor, and marvel at the Beaux-Arts architecture.

4. Stroll to Rockefeller Center: Make your way to Rockefeller Center, a complex of commercial buildings that is home to NBC Studios, Radio City Music Hall, and the famous ice-skating rink during winter. Don't forget to visit the Top of the Rock observation deck for stunning views of the city.

5. Explore St. Patrick's Cathedral: Just across from Rockefeller Center, St. Patrick's Cathedral is a neo-Gothic Roman Catholic cathedral that is both an architectural and spiritual landmark in New York City.

6. Stop by Radio City Music Hall: As you continue your tour, visit Radio City Music Hall, an entertainment venue that is home to the world-famous Rockettes and hosts numerous concerts, events, and the annual Christmas Spectacular.

7. End at Times Square: Conclude your walking tour at the bustling and vibrant Times Square, often referred to as "The Crossroads of the World." Surrounded by bright billboards, theaters, shops, and restaurants, Times Square is the perfect place to immerse yourself in the energy of New York City.

This walking tour will give you a taste of some of Manhattan's most iconic landmarks, helping you get acquainted with the city's energy and history during your first day in the Big Apple.

Suggested Second Day Walking Tour:

Start your day by visiting Hudson Yards, an impressive, modern development on Manhattan's West Side. From there, head to the High Line, a beautiful, elevated park built on former railroad tracks. As you walk along the High Line, take in the urban greenery and unique views of the city.

Once you reach the end of the High Line, make your way to Chelsea Market, a popular indoor market known for its diverse food offerings and trendy shops. Here, you can grab a bite to eat from one of the many delicious vendors or do some shopping.

After you've explored Chelsea Market, continue your journey to the famous Carrie Bradshaw apartment from the "Sex and the City" series. Located in Greenwich Village, the picturesque brownstone is a must-see for fans of the show.

Following your visit to the apartment, head to O Cafe in Midtown. This relaxed, Brazilian-inspired cafe is perfect for people-watching on Sixth Avenue and offers excellent coffee, lemon cake, and salads.

Next, make your way to Central Park, the iconic green oasis in the heart of Manhattan. Take a leisurely stroll through the park, enjoy its many attractions, and perhaps rent a bike or a boat to further explore the area.

Finally, stop by the Dakota Building, located just outside Central Park at 72nd Street. This historic cooperative building is famous for its association with John Lennon and Yoko Ono.

Throughout your day, be sure to sample the variety of culinary delights available at Chelsea Market and enjoy a refreshing coffee break at O Cafe.

11.5 Best Budget-Friendly Dining Options in Manhattan

Shake Shack Burgers: This popular burger chain has multiple locations in Manhattan, offering single burgers for $5.69 and double burgers for $8.49. Be prepared for queues during peak hours, but you can download the Shack app to pre-order and skip the wait. Wi-Fi is not provided in the stores.

Taim for Falafel: Located in Little Italy, Taim offers delicious falafel wraps ($7.75), salads ($10), and mezzes ($6-$7). Try the green falafel in pita.

Midtown Budget Food Recommendations:

- Best Burgers: Shake Shack, Burger Joint (multiple locations)
- Best Pizza: Joe's Pizza (try the supreme for $4.75), 2 Bros Pizza (try the margarita for $1)
- Best Sushi: Wasabi Sushi Bento near Times Square
- Best Cuban Sandwich: Margon
- Street Food: Visit http://roaminghunger.com/food-trucks/ny/new-york/ to find the best food trucks and their locations.
- Best Cheesecake: Junior's Cheesecake near Times Square ($9 for a large slice)
- Best Brunch: Sadelle's, Balthazar, Epistrophy, Two Hands

Top Dinner Recommendation:

La Esquina: This popular Mexican restaurant offers a great ambiance and food, but it can be pricey and difficult to book. Make reservations early on OpenTable, or check for cancellations and last-minute slots. While the dining experience is great, be prepared for a 70-90 minute time limit per table.

Best Casual Bar:

Please Don't Tell (PDT): A cozy bar with great cocktails and some food. Call at 3 pm for a reservation, or be prepared for a 1-3 hour wait. The entrance is through a phone booth.

11.6 NYC Passes To Purchase Before You Go to NYC

New York City is filled with must-see attractions, such as the Empire State Building, Rockefeller Center, Statue of Liberty, Central Park, MoMA, and the Brooklyn Bridge. However, visiting these popular sites can involve long queues, particularly during peak season from April to September, and the ticket prices can quickly add up. To save time and money, consider purchasing a pass before your trip. While going with the flow might sound appealing, it's not always feasible in NYC.

Here are some pass options to help you make the most of your visit. Keep in mind that it's essential to calculate whether purchasing a pass is worth it based on the number of attractions you plan to visit. We've listed the most popular passes so you can explore and decide for yourself:

[1. New York City Explorer Pass. (Book it Here)](#)

The New York City Explorer Pass offers access to 56 attractions, allowing you to choose from 3, 5, 7, or 10 top attractions and tours in New York. This pass helps you save up to 45% compared to regular admission prices. You don't need to decide in advance, and the pass is valid for 30 days. The cost is 85 USD per person.

The New York attractions you can select include:
Top of the Rock, Empire State Building, Statue of Liberty Ferry Ticket, · Hop-On Hop-Off Downtown Tour by CitySights, American Museum of Natural History, Ripley's Believe it or Not! including Impossible LaseRace!, Museum of Modern Art, Metropolitan Museum of Art, Circle Line 2-Hour Semi-Circle Cruise, Guggenheim Museum, NY Water Taxi Statue By Night Cruise, Intrepid Sea, Air & Space Museum, CitySights Brooklyn Tour, CitySights Uptown Treasures & Harlem Hop-On Hop-Off Tour, Body Worlds: Pulse at Discovery Times Square, Star Wars and the Power of Costume at

Discovery Times Square, NY TV and Movie Sites Tour by On Location Tours, 90-Minute Midtown Cruise by City Sightseeing Cruises, Radio City Music Hall Stage Door Tour, Museum of Sex, Rockefeller Center Tour, CitySights Multilingual Upper and Lower Manhattan Tour, Night Tour, 90-Minute Twilight Cruise by City Sightseeing Cruises, National 9/11 Memorial with Hop on Hop off Water Taxi, Circle Line Liberty Cruise, Gossip Girl Tour by On Location Tours,· Food On Foot Tours, New York Historical Society Museum, 9/11 Tribute Center and Guided Tour, Lincoln Center for the Performing Arts Guided Tour, Full-Day Bike Rental, NY Botanical Garden All Garden Pass, Central Park Movie Tour by On Location Tours, Brooklyn Bridge and DUMBO Neighborhood Tour, Brooklyn Museum and Brooklyn Botanic Garden, SHARK Speedboat Thrill Ride, The Shearwater Classic Schooner, Manhattan by Sail: Clipper City Tall Ship (seasonal), Circle Line Beast Speedboat Ride, 3-Hour Full Island Cruise by Circle Line Sightseeing Cruises, NYC Water Taxi Hop On Hop Off All Day Pass, Madison Square Garden Tour, Madison Square Garden: MSG All-Access Tour, Central Park Sightseeing: Central Park Tour, Brooklyn Bridge Sightseeing: Brooklyn Bridge Tour, Brooklyn Bridge Sightseeing: Full-Day Bike Rental, On Location Tours: Soprano's Tour, Statue of Liberty Cruise Express Cruise, Woodbury Commons Premium Outlet Shopping Trip, Yankee Stadium: Classic Tour, Luna Park at Coney Island: 4-hour unlimited ride wristband (seasonal),Whitney Museum of American Art, The RIDE, The TOUR, Senor Frogs: 3-course dining menu, plus souvenir, and express seating, When Harry Met Seinfeld Bus Tour (choice of 1 On Location Bus Tour), Central Park Walking Tour, Star Wars & the Power of Costume Exhibit at Discovery Times Square (limited time through September 20, 2016), The Vikings Exhibition at Discovery Times Square (limited time through September 20, 2016)

2. NYC it All: 4 in 1 Sightseeing Combination Ticket (Book it Here)

With this ticket, you combine 4 activities in NYC. On this combination, you'll visit the (1) Empire State Building Observatory and the (2) Metropolitan Museum of Art. You also get a ride around the city on a (3) hop-on-hop-off tour and see Manhattan from the water on your choice of a

(4) Harbor Lights or Statue of Liberty cruise. It costs 90 EUR (118 USD) per person.

3. NYC Freestyle Pass with 3 or 5 Attractions (Book it Here)

This combo ticket will help you to see New York on your own terms with a 72-hour Hop-on Hop-off Bus ticket and your choice of either 3 or 5 iconic attractions. It costs 127 EUR (150USD) per person. More info and bookings here.

4. NYC Downtown Experience Combo Package (Book it Here).

This combo ticket will help you to discover the best of Downtown New York with a 24-hour combo package and get access to both the hop-on and hop-off sightseeing bus and a hop-on and hop-off ferry cruise. Get a ticket to the One World Observatory and 911 Tribute Center. More info and bookings here.

11.7 How Expensive is Manhattan

Manhattan, the bustling heart of New York City, is known for its vibrant culture, iconic landmarks, and exceptional dining experiences. However, it's also known for being one of the more expensive cities in the United States. To help you plan your trip and manage your expenses, we've compiled a list of estimated costs for various necessities during your visit to Manhattan.

Food:

- Breakfast: $7 - $15 per person
- Lunch: $12 - $25 per person
- Dinner: $20 - $50 per person (depending on the restaurant)
- Snacks: $5 - $10 per person

Transportation:

- MetroCard (subway and bus): $2.75 per ride, $33 for a 7-day unlimited pass
- Yellow taxi: Initial charge $2.50, $2.50 per mile, plus waiting time
- Ride-sharing apps: $10 - $25 per ride (depending on distance and demand)

Drinks:

- Bottle of water: $1 - $3
- Soft drinks: $2 - $4
- Coffee: $3 - $6
- Alcoholic drinks: $8 - $15 (depending on the venue)

Accommodations:

- Mid-range hotel: $150 - $300 per night (depending on the season and location)

Attractions:

- Museums: $15 - $25 per person (some offer free admission on specific days or suggested donation policies)
- Guided tours: $25 - $50 per person
- Theater tickets: $30 - $200 per person (depending on the show and seat location)

Miscellaneous:

- Souvenirs: $5 - $50
- Tips: 15 - 20% of the bill at restaurants and $1 - $2 per bag for hotel porters

Estimated Daily Budget for a Couple:

Considering the costs mentioned above, a couple can expect to spend approximately $250 - $400 per day for a mid-range experience in Manhattan. This includes accommodations, meals, transportation, attractions, and miscellaneous expenses. Keep in mind that this is a rough estimate, and your actual expenses may vary depending on your preferences and itinerary.

Remember that there are many ways to save money in Manhattan, such as using public transportation, taking advantage of free or discounted museum admissions, and enjoying the numerous free attractions, parks, and events throughout the city. Planning your trip carefully and prioritizing your expenses can help you make the most of your Manhattan adventure without breaking the bank.

11.8 Bucket List

New York City, the city that never sleeps, has an endless array of experiences waiting for you to explore. In just a few days, you can discover the rich culture, iconic landmarks, and vibrant atmosphere that make NYC truly unique. From world-class museums and iconic bridges to stunning parks and dazzling Broadway shows, this bucket list highlights the must-see attractions and experiences that will make your visit to the Big Apple truly unforgettable. So, pack your bags and get ready to immerse yourself in the sights, sounds, and flavors of New York City!

- Visit the MOMA museum

- Walk the Brooklyn Bridge

- Go up the Empire State Building, Top of the Rock, or One World Trade Center

- Explore Central Park (walk, bike, or run)

- Take a photo of the Statue of Liberty

- See the Flatiron Building

- Enjoy a live jazz performance at a jazz bar
- Attend a Broadway show
- Stroll along the High Line Park
- Visit Chelsea Market and grab a bite to eat
- Experience Times Square
- Explore the New York Public Library
- Marvel at Grand Central Station
- Shop at your favorite stores
- Dine at La Esquina
- Go clubbing at Le Bain
- Snap a photo touching the Charging Bull on Wall Street
- Savor coffee and shop in Soho
- Take a photo at Carrie Bradshaw's apartment

12. Customized Itineraries

12.1 3-Day, 5-Day, and 7-Day Itineraries

When planning a trip to New York City, it's essential to create an itinerary that allows you to experience the best the city has to offer. Whether you have three, five, or seven days to explore, these suggested itineraries will ensure you make the most of your time in the Big Apple.

12.1.1 3-Day Itinerary

Day 1:

Morning: Visit the Statue of Liberty and Ellis Island

- 08:00 - Start your day by taking the subway to Battery Park, where you will board the ferry to the Statue of Liberty and Ellis Island. The nearest subway station is Bowling Green (4, 5 lines) or South Ferry (1 line). Arrive early to avoid long lines and allow enough time for security checks. Purchase tickets in advance through the official website (www.statuecruises.com) to secure your spot. Prices for adults are $23.50, seniors (62+) are $18, and children (4-12) are $12.
- 09:00 - Board the ferry to the Statue of Liberty, which includes an audio tour. Take your time exploring Liberty Island, then board the next ferry to Ellis Island.
- 11:00 - Arrive at Ellis Island, where you can visit the Immigration Museum and learn about the history of immigration in the United States. Consider renting an audio guide for a more immersive experience.

Afternoon: Explore the Financial District, including Wall Street and the Charging Bull

- 13:00 - Return to Battery Park via ferry and begin exploring the Financial District. Head to Wall Street, the heart of the financial world, and admire the New York Stock Exchange building.

- 13:30 - Walk a few blocks south to find the Charging Bull, a famous bronze statue symbolizing the strength and determination of the American people. Snap a picture with the bull before continuing your exploration.
- 14:00 - Take a lunch break at one of the many nearby restaurants or cafes in the Financial District.
- 15:00 - After lunch, you can visit other attractions in the area, such as the 9/11 Memorial and One World Trade Center. To get there, walk about 10 minutes west from the Charging Bull.

Evening: Experience the bright lights of Times Square and catch a Broadway show

- 17:00 - Head to Times Square by taking the subway from the nearby Fulton Street Station (A, C, J, Z, 2, 3, 4, or 5 lines) or World Trade Center (E line) to Times Square-42nd Street Station. Marvel at the dazzling lights and electronic billboards that make this area an iconic part of New York City.
- 18:30 - Have dinner at one of the many restaurants in the Times Square area. Make sure to factor in enough time to get to your Broadway show.
- 20:00 - Attend a Broadway show at one of the many theaters in the area. Book your tickets in advance online or at the box office, or try your luck at the TKTS Booth in Times Square for discounted same-day tickets.
- 22:30 - After the show, take a leisurely stroll through Times Square, which is still bustling with activity at this hour.
- 23:00 - End your day by taking the subway back to your accommodation. Use the Times Square-42nd Street Station to board the appropriate line for your destination.

Day 2:

Morning: Stroll through Central Park and visit the Dakota Building

- 08:00 - Start your day by taking the subway to Central Park. You can use either the 59th Street-Columbus Circle Station (A, B, C, D, or 1 lines) or the 72nd Street Station (B, C lines) to access the park.
- 09:00 - Begin your stroll through Central Park, enjoying its lush greenery, picturesque bridges, and serene ponds. Some highlights include the Bethesda Terrace, Bow Bridge, and the Alice in Wonderland statue.
- 10:30 - Make your way to the Dakota Building, located just outside Central Park West and 72nd Street. This historic building is famous for being the home of John Lennon and the site of his tragic assassination. Take a moment to visit the nearby Strawberry Fields memorial in his honor.

Afternoon: Discover the Museum of Modern Art (MoMA) and Rockefeller Center

- 12:00 - Head to the Museum of Modern Art (MoMA) by taking the subway from the 72nd Street Station (B, C lines) to the 47-50 Streets-Rockefeller Center Station (B, D, F, or M lines). The entrance fee for adults is $25, seniors (65+) are $18, and students are $14. Children under 16 are free.
- 12:30 - Explore the MoMA's vast collection of contemporary and modern art, including works by famous artists such as Picasso, Van Gogh, and Warhol.
- 15:00 - Take a short walk from MoMA to Rockefeller Center, a famous New York City landmark featuring the iconic Prometheus statue, Radio City Music Hall, and the iconic ice-skating rink during winter months.
- 15:30 - Grab a bite to eat at one of the many restaurants or cafes in the Rockefeller Center area.

Evening: Go up the Empire State Building or Top of the Rock for stunning city views

- 17:00 - Choose between the Empire State Building or Top of the Rock for breathtaking city views. The Empire State Building is a short walk from the 34th Street-Herald Square Station (B, D, F, M, N, Q, R, or W lines), while Top of the Rock is located within Rockefeller Center.
- 18:00 - For the Empire State Building, purchase tickets in advance on their website or at the ticket office. Prices range from $42 for adults, $40 for seniors, and $36 for children. For Top of the Rock, tickets are $36 for adults, $34 for seniors, and $30 for children. It's recommended to book a timed ticket in advance.
- 19:30 - After taking in the views, have dinner at a nearby restaurant, enjoying the culinary delights that New York City has to offer.
- 21:00 - End your day by taking the subway back to your accommodation. Use either the 34th Street-Herald Square Station (for Empire State Building) or the 47-50 Streets-Rockefeller Center Station (for Top of the Rock) to board the appropriate line for your destination.

Day 3:

Morning: Walk the Brooklyn Bridge and explore DUMBO

- 08:00 - Start your day by taking the subway to the Brooklyn Bridge-City Hall Station (4, 5, 6, J, or Z lines) or the High Street-Brooklyn Bridge Station (A or C lines), depending on which side of the bridge you'd like to begin your walk.
- 09:00 - Begin your walk across the iconic Brooklyn Bridge, taking in the stunning views of Manhattan's skyline and the East River.
- 10:00 - After crossing the bridge, explore DUMBO (Down Under the Manhattan Bridge Overpass), a trendy neighborhood known for its art galleries, boutiques, and beautiful waterfront parks, such as Brooklyn Bridge Park and Jane's Carousel.

Afternoon: Wander through the neighborhoods of SoHo and Greenwich Village

- 12:00 - Head back to Manhattan and take the subway from the High Street-Brooklyn Bridge Station (A or C lines) to the West 4th Street-Washington Square Station (A, B, C, D, E, F, or M lines).
- 12:30 - Explore the fashionable neighborhood of SoHo, known for its stylish boutiques, art galleries, and historic cast-iron buildings.
- 14:00 - Continue your exploration in Greenwich Village, a bohemian neighborhood with charming streets, unique shops, and Washington Square Park as its centerpiece.
- 15:30 - Grab a coffee or snack at one of the many cafes in the area.

Evening: Enjoy dinner at La Esquina and experience the nightlife at a jazz bar or club like Le Bain

- 18:00 - Head to La Esquina (114 Kenmare St, New York, NY 10012), a popular Mexican restaurant known for its delicious tacos and vibrant atmosphere. Reservations are recommended, as the place can get busy.
- 20:00 - After dinner, make your way to a jazz bar or club to experience New York City's nightlife. For a jazz bar, consider Smalls Jazz Club (183 W 10th St, New York, NY 10014) or Blue Note (131 W 3rd St, New York, NY 10012). If you prefer a club, check out Le Bain (848 Washington St, New York, NY 10014), a rooftop bar and nightclub with stunning views.
- 23:00 - End your day by taking the subway or a taxi back to your accommodation. Be sure to check the subway lines and schedules for late-night service changes.

12.1.2 5-Day Itinerary

In addition to the 3-day itinerary, add:

Day 4:

Morning: Visit the Metropolitan Museum of Art or the American Museum of Natural History

08:00 - Start your day by choosing either the Metropolitan Museum of Art (1000 5th Ave, New York, NY 10028) or the American Museum of Natural History (Central Park West & 79th St, New York, NY 10024). Both museums open at 10:00 am, but arrive early to beat the crowds.

To reach the Metropolitan Museum of Art, take the 4, 5, or 6 subway lines to the 86th Street station and walk to the museum. For the American Museum of Natural History, take the B or C subway lines to the 81st Street-Museum of Natural History station.

Afternoon: Explore Chelsea Market and walk the High Line Park

- 12:30 - Take the subway to the 14th Street-8th Avenue Station (A, C, E, or L lines) and walk to Chelsea Market (75 9th Ave, New York, NY 10011), a popular indoor food market and shopping destination.
- 14:00 - After browsing Chelsea Market, head to the nearby High Line Park, a beautiful elevated park built on a former railway line. The park stretches from Gansevoort Street to 34th Street, offering stunning views of the city and a peaceful place to stroll.

Evening: Check out a comedy club or live music venue in the East Village or Lower East Side

- 17:30 - Make your way to the East Village or Lower East Side by taking the subway to the 1st Avenue Station (L line) or the 2nd Avenue Station (F or M lines).
- 18:30 - Grab dinner at one of the many restaurants in the area, offering diverse culinary options from Italian to Japanese and everything in between.
- 20:00 - Check out a comedy club or live music venue for a fun night out. For comedy, consider the Comedy Cellar (117 Macdougal St, New York, NY 10012) or the Upright Citizens Brigade Theatre (555 W 42nd St, New York, NY 10036). For live music, visit the Bowery Ballroom (6 Delancey

St, New York, NY 10002) or Rockwood Music Hall (196 Allen St, New York, NY 10002).
- 23:00 - End your day by taking the subway or a taxi back to your accommodation. Be sure to check the subway lines and schedules for late-night service changes.

Day 5:

• Morning: Tour the **Grand Central Terminal** and **New York Public Library**

08:00 - Start your day at the Grand Central Terminal (89 E 42nd St, New York, NY 10017). Take the 4, 5, 6, 7, or S subway lines to the Grand Central-42nd Street station. Walk around the iconic terminal, marvel at its architecture, and enjoy breakfast at one of the many food options available.

10:00 - Head to the New York Public Library (476 5th Ave, New York, NY 10018), just a 10-minute walk from Grand Central. Explore the beautiful Rose Main Reading Room and the various exhibits on display.

• Afternoon: Discover the iconic **Flatiron Building** and relax in **Madison Square Park**

12:30 - Walk from the New York Public Library to the Flatiron Building (175 5th Ave, New York, NY 10010), a 20-minute walk. Snap some photos of the iconic building before heading to Madison Square Park, just across the street.

13:00 - Relax in Madison Square Park, grab lunch at one of the nearby restaurants or food kiosks, and enjoy the green space and art installations.

• Evening: Take a **sunset cruise** around Manhattan or attend a **sports event** at Madison Square Garden or Yankee Stadium

16:00 - Choose between a sunset cruise around Manhattan or attending a sports event. For a sunset cruise, head to the pier where your chosen cruise departs (check the company's website for pier location and departure time). Book your tickets in advance and arrive early to ensure a spot.

For a sports event, head to either Madison Square Garden (4 Pennsylvania Plaza, New York, NY 10001) or Yankee Stadium (1 E 161 St, The Bronx, NY 10451). Check the event schedules and book tickets in advance. To reach Madison Square Garden, take the 1, 2, 3, A, C, or E subway lines to the 34th Street-Penn Station. For Yankee Stadium, take the 4, B, or D subway lines to the 161st Street-Yankee Stadium station.

23:00 - End your day by taking the subway or a taxi back to your accommodation. Be sure to check the subway lines and schedules for late-night service changes.

12.1.3 7-Day Itinerary

In addition to the 5-day itinerary, add:

Day 6:

- Morning: Explore the neighborhoods of **Williamsburg, Brooklyn** and **Flushing, Queens**

08:00 - Start your day in Williamsburg, Brooklyn. Take the L subway line to Bedford Avenue station. Wander around the neighborhood, enjoy the street art, and have breakfast at a local café or bakery.

10:30 - Head to Flushing, Queens, which is known for its vibrant Asian community. Take the 7 subway line to Flushing-Main Street station. Explore the bustling streets, shops, and markets.

- Afternoon: Visit the **Bronx Zoo** or the **New York Botanical Garden**

13:00 - Choose between visiting the Bronx Zoo (2300 Southern Blvd, The Bronx, NY 10460) or the New York Botanical Garden (2900 Southern Blvd, The Bronx, NY 10458). Both attractions are located in the Bronx and are accessible via public transportation. For the Bronx Zoo, take the 2 or 5 subway lines to West Farms Square-East Tremont Avenue station. For the

New York Botanical Garden, take the B, D, or 4 subway lines to Bedford Park Blvd station, then transfer to the Bx26 bus towards Co-op City. Check their websites for opening hours and ticket prices. Make sure to book tickets in advance.

• Evening: Sample diverse cuisine in one of NYC's ethnic enclaves like **Little Italy** or **Chinatown**

18:00 - Head to either Little Italy or Chinatown in Manhattan for dinner. To reach Little Italy, take the 6 subway line to Spring Street or Canal Street station. To reach Chinatown, take the N, Q, R, W, J, or Z subway lines to Canal Street station. Stroll around, soak up the atmosphere, and choose from a variety of restaurants offering authentic ethnic cuisine.

23:00 - End your day by taking the subway or a taxi back to your accommodation. Be sure to check the subway lines and schedules for late-night service changes.

Day 7:

• Morning: Take a bike ride along the **Hudson River Greenway**

08:00 - Start your day by renting a bike from a nearby bike rental shop or use a Citi Bike, which is available throughout Manhattan. Begin your ride at Battery Park in lower Manhattan and follow the Hudson River Greenway, a dedicated bike path that runs along the Hudson River. Enjoy the scenic views and stop at various parks and piers along the way.

• Afternoon: Visit the **9/11 Memorial and Museum** or the **One World Observatory**

13:00 - Make your way to the World Trade Center site. Choose between visiting the 9/11 Memorial and Museum (180 Greenwich St, New York, NY 10007) or the One World Observatory (285 Fulton St, New York, NY 10007). For the 9/11 Memorial and Museum, be sure to book tickets in advance on their website. For the One World Observatory, tickets can be purchased online or on-site, but pre-booking is recommended. Both attractions are accessible via multiple subway lines; take the A, C, 1, 2, 3, 4, 5, J, or Z to Fulton Street station or the E to World Trade Center station.

• Evening: Unwind in a rooftop bar with panoramic city views and reflect on your unforgettable NYC adventure

18:00 - Cap off your New York City experience by visiting a rooftop bar with stunning city views. Some options include 230 Fifth Rooftop Bar (230 5th Ave, New York, NY 10001), The Press Lounge (653 11th Ave, New York, NY 10036), or The Ides at Wythe Hotel (80 Wythe Ave, Brooklyn, NY 11249). To reach these locations, use subway lines or taxis/rideshare services. Be aware of dress codes and age restrictions at some venues. Enjoy a drink, take in the view, and reminisce on your amazing NYC adventure.

23:00 - End your evening by returning to your accommodation via subway or taxi/rideshare. Be sure to check the subway lines and schedules for late-night service changes.

Remember that these itineraries are just suggestions, and you can mix and match or customize them to suit your interests and preferences. No matter how long you have to spend in New York City, you're sure to create lasting memories in this vibrant and exciting metropolis.

Online Maps with all the Locations of the 7-Day Travel Itinerary

We have compiled all the locations of the 7-day travel itinerary for New York City on Google Maps, conveniently grouped by day to enhance your travel experience. By accessing the personalized map below, you can visualize each day's destinations, calculate distances and travel times, and explore nearby attractions, restaurants, and accommodations with ease. This custom map not only streamlines your planning process but also ensures that everyone in your travel group is on the same page. Make the most of your time in the city by taking advantage of this comprehensive Google Maps resource, which allows you to focus on enjoying all the incredible sights and experiences that New York City has to offer. Access

the map below to start planning your unforgettable adventure.

https://www.google.com/maps/d/edit?mid=1CYJxI5Rcf_IXcO4udDpIMiAcbVq_aSg&usp=sharing

Here is an easier link if you are an offline reader: http://bit.ly/40gCRfr

or alternatively you can scan the below barcode with your camera.

Our Detailed 3-Day Travel Itinerary to NYC and Manhattan

Embarking on a journey to New York City, the bustling metropolis of dreams and iconic landmarks, can be an overwhelming yet thrilling experience. To help you navigate the vibrant streets of Manhattan and make the most of your three-day trip, we have crafted a detailed itinerary that highlights the best attractions, dining, and cultural experiences that the city has to offer. With our carefully curated guide, you'll be able to immerse yourself in the essence of NYC, ticking off bucket-list-worthy sites, and making lasting memories in the city that never sleeps. Get ready to embark on a whirlwind adventure through the heart of Manhattan, where every corner brings new discoveries and delights.

Day 1 in NYC: Arrival

10:00 Arrival in New York City at LaGuardia Or JFK International.
Public transportation and taxis are available for travel to the hotel.

10:30 Transportation from the Airport to the Hotel
Take the public transportation or a taxi to Club Quarters Downtown 52 Williams St. New York, NY 10005

Costs: $2.50 by train/person, $45 by taxi from LaGuardia, $50 by taxi from JFK. You can also use Uber or Lyft (View ZoomTip 1.1)

11:30 Arrive and check into your hotel.
It will take about an hour on public transportation to reach the hotel from LaGuardia, 40 minutes by taxi. It will take about an hour on public transportation and about an hour by taxi from JFK International.

12:00 Grab a bite to eat at Pound & Pence 55 Liberty St.
The restaurant is 3 minutes' walking distance from the hotel and has a great atmosphere along with great food. It's more like a British pub, and people come here usually after their work. The most popular times are

around 6 PM to 7 PM. It's ok in the noon, at around 12 AM, but not full of people. They serve great burgers and many excellent beers from the tap. On Monday's nights, there is an offer for 2 for 1 drinks or beers.

Cost: $10 - $25/person

2 Pound and Pence Restaurant

13:00 Visit the Statue of Liberty

After having a bite to eat, you can start your NYC adventure with a trip to the Statue of Liberty. You can explore the Financial District while you take a walk to Battery Park, where the ferry departs from.

Cost: Statue of Liberty ferry tickets: $18/person

View ZoomTip 1.2

3 The famous Statue of Liberty

15:10 Explore the Famous Times Square.

Be sure to stop by Ripley's Odditorium and Madame Tussaud's Wax Museum. Other attractions include Dave & Busters and The Hard Rock Café

4 Ripley's Believe it or Not Odditorium

Ripley's Believe It or Not Odditorium
Location: 234 W 42nd St, New York, NY 10036
Hours of Operation: Open daily from 9 AM to 1 AM
Official Website: http://www.ripleysnewyork.com/
Admission Fee: $30 per person
Visitor's Review: This attraction is not your typical amusement park. Instead, it's more of an educational museum where visitors are encouraged to take their time and learn fascinating facts. Don't anticipate passive entertainment here.

5 Madame Tussaud's Wax museum offers you the chance to meet many celebrities..but in their wax format

Madame Tussaud's Wax Museum
Address: 234 W 42nd St, New York, NY 10036
Opening Times: Friday and Saturday from 10 AM to 10 PM, All other days from 10 AM to 8 PM
Website: https://www.madametussauds.com/new-york/en/
Review: It's a fun experience especially if you have never been to a Wax museum before. If you have already been in a wax museum, skip it; you will not gain anything new.
Cost: 36 USD per person. The digital photos of you and your family shot by the museum cost 15 USD per photo, so be careful of the pricing.

19:00 Dinner at The Jekyll & Hyde Club

Headed back towards downtown, Jekyll & Hyde is an experience, to say the least. Served by a host of unusual characters, be prepared for a one-of-a-kind dinner.

7 The Jekyll and Hyde Restaurant and Bar in NYC

Jekyll and Hyde Restaurant
Address: 91 7th Ave S, New York, NY 10014
Opening Times: Friday and Saturday from 12 PM to 2 AM. All other days from 12 PM to 12 AM.
Menu: http://places.singleplatform.com/jekyll--hyde/menu
Website: http://www.jekyllandhydeclub.com/
Review: Well, the food here is not the best in NYC, to be honest. So, don't have high expectations on the food side. It is also pricey. You come here for the fun and the experience. There is a 3 USD charge per person for the entertainment part.
Cost: $30 - $40 / person

21:00 Attend a performance at the Upright Citizens Brigade, a renowned comedy club in the nation.

Multiple shows take place every night, offering ample opportunities to enjoy comedians showcasing their finest work. Admission Fee: Free - $10/person Location: 307 W 26th St, New York, NY 10001 Helpful Hints: Reasonably priced beers and drinks are available. Arrive early, as long lines often form; for example, if a popular show starts at 9 PM, people may begin queuing as early as 6 PM. Audience interaction is a common feature, and the best comedy troupes typically perform on weekends. Entry prices range from free to $5-$10 per person.

8 A comedy club - Upright Citizens Brigade Theatre

23:00 Return to the hotel and unwind

Going back to your hotel doesn't signify the end of your night. The hotel features a full-service restaurant and bar, a 24-hour fitness center, and an exclusive club living room, providing various activities without the need to venture out.

Cost: $2.50/person

Lower Manhattan 1st Day Map

Below you can find your online Google Map, with all the suggested destinations for your first day in NYC. It will help you to navigate quickly to all of them when you are in NYC. You can click on the photo or on the link below to get it.

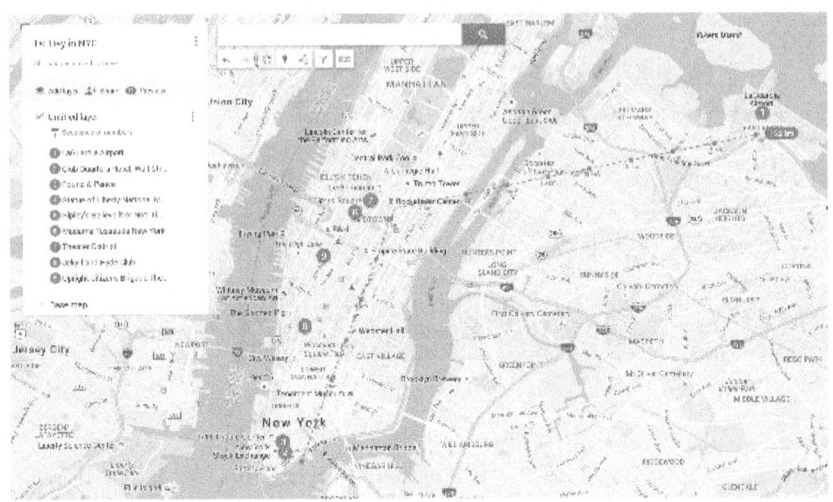

9 The Online Google Map for the 1st Day in NYC Itinerary

You can get this map online at
https://drive.google.com/open?id=1dMMvaliR_YAOCjDC42OvdErDjvg&usp=sharing

Zooming on: Transportation

There are multiple ways to reach Manhattan from LaGuardia and JFK International airports, depending on your budget and available time. We prefer public transportation due to the significant cost savings it offers, and it operates 24/7 in New York City.

LaGuardia: *Change machines are available in the terminal. Ask an agent for directions. You'll need $2.50 per person for the bus fare. Upon exiting the terminal, follow the signs for the various buses that serve the airport. Take the M60 bus, which crosses the bridge into Manhattan at 125th street. *Luggage racks are provided on the bus for your convenience. Using them makes the ride more comfortable, especially when the bus is crowded. Disembark the bus at West 125th Street and Lenox Avenue to catch the #2 or #3 train. *Inform the bus driver of your destination, and they'll gladly inform you when you've reached your stop. Alternatively, remember to get off in front of the CVS.

Other options for traveling from LaGuardia or JFK International to your hotel: At the corner where you got off the bus, you'll find the downtown train station entrance. Head downstairs and purchase a MetroCard. We recommend two $20 MetroCards, which will cover multiple trips and can be refilled when empty. Both the #2 and #3 trains stop at this station, and either one will work for your journey. Get off the train at Wall St., at the intersection of Pine St and William St. From there, it's a short walk to 52 William St.

Taxi: Taxi stands can be found near most airport exits. An attendant will provide you with a paper indicating the estimated cost of your trip.

Shared Airport Shuttles to General NYC Locations: Several companies offer shared shuttle services to various locations in the city, but they may not take you directly to your specific destination. In such cases, you would need to take a taxi or train from the drop-off point. This option isn't our top recommendation.

Hotel-specific Airport Shuttles: A more convenient alternative to shared shuttles is booking a private van that takes you directly to your hotel. This service can be booked for around 20 USD (18 EUR) per person - you can

book one here,

10 The Go Airlink Shuttle costs 20 USD (18 EUR) per person and gets you from the Airports of NYC to your hotel.

Private Luxury Car: If you're looking to indulge, opt for a private luxury car transfer. With this service, you'll enjoy a personal chauffeur and a high-end vehicle, bypassing any taxi queues. The cost is 120 USD (97 EUR) for three people (approximately 40 USD per person), and reservations can be made here (book it here)

Note: City buses require exact change or a Metrocard for payment. Pennies are not accepted.

Where can I find Currency Exchanges and Cash Machines (ATMs)? A currency exchange is conveniently located in the heart of Times Square, next to Dave & Busters. ATMs can be found at various points in the airport, grocery stores, and chain pharmacy stores (Rite Aid, CVS, etc.) throughout the city.

How to reach the Airport to City Bus Exit the terminal and follow signs for the M60 bus.

JFK Airport to your Hotel in Manhattan with Lyft Lyft is often slightly more affordable than Uber, typically being 5-10% cheaper. It appears that more drivers in NYC prefer Lyft, so you may want to download and use the app. For one person, the Lyft price from JFK to central Manhattan is around 38 USD, and you add 5 USD for a second passenger, making it 43 USD for two people. However, you will have to share the ride with another passenger. The price fluctuates based on demand and supply.

To use Lyft, download the app and set your terminal and passenger pickup location. For example, Terminal 4 is where international flights arrive. Upon exiting the arrivals terminal, you will see signs directing you to the passenger pickup spots (e.g., "Passenger Pick up D"). Then, you wait. The app isn't perfect – sometimes, your driver may arrive and leave without notifying you, requiring you to wait for a new driver. The wait time is usually around 5-6 minutes. Keep in mind that there is no shelter at the passenger pickup locations if the weather is unfavorable.

A private Lyft ride without sharing will cost around 55 USD, while a regular taxi is approximately 65 USD. Lyft vehicles are often Toyota Camry or Prius models. The trip from JFK to Fifth Avenue, Midtown Manhattan, takes about 50 minutes. Tipping Lyft and Uber drivers is not typically expected, but regular taxi drivers should receive a 15-20% tip. Lyft cars are usually clean, offer phone chargers, and may even accommodate a quick food stop en route to your hotel.

An important note about Lyft in NYC: Once you confirm a driver will pick you up (e.g., from your hotel to the airport) and they are scheduled to arrive in 10 minutes, you might experience the driver canceling and another driver taking their place. This could happen multiple times in a row, resulting in a 30-minute wait. To avoid this, call the first driver upon confirmation and ask them to verify if they will pick you up. You may also want to check with Uber for better response times. Uber prices are similar to Lyft.

Zooming on: Public Transportation Directions Day 1

Times Square

To reach Times Square, take the uptown #1 train to 14th Street. Transfer to the #2 train platform and continue to 42nd Street. Choose any exit to explore different parts of Times Square.

MetroCard: $2.50/person

Jekyll and Hyde Club 91 7th Avenue South

To get there, take the downtown #2 train to Christopher Street. Exit near the intersection of Grove St & 7th Avenue South. The restaurant is just up the block.

Upright Citizens Brigade, 153 East 3rd Street

To get there, take the uptown #2 train to 14th Street. Exit near the intersection of West 14th Street and Avenue of the Americas (6th Avenue). Walk east on West 14th Street. Then, take the M14A bus going towards Grand-FDR and get off at Avenue A and East 3rd Street. Walk towards East 3rd Street, turn right, and the venue is up the block.

Club Quarters - Wall Street, 52 William Street

To reach the hotel, take a taxi. The ride should take about 10 minutes and cost no more than $12.00.

Day 2 in NYC: Shopping, Famous Restaurants & More

09:00 Breakfast in Herald Square at Tick Tock Dinner 481 8th avenue and shopping at Macy's

New York City boasts many iconic restaurants and diners, including the Tick Tock Diner. Situated on 34th Street, it's nestled in the heart of a bustling shopping district where you can easily spend hours exploring.

Cost: $10 - $20/person

12:00 Enjoy a Sandwich at Tick Tock Diner

Tick Tock Diner, Address: The New Yorker, A Wyndham Hotel, 481 8th Ave, New York, Opening Times: 24 hours, Website: http://ticktockdinerny.com/beta2015/

Review: The Tick Tock Diner is a decent spot for a quick bite. While not extraordinary, the diner offers fair prices and satisfactory food quality.

11:00 Take a ride IN the Empire State Building

The Empire State Building offers a variety of attractions for visitors to enjoy. Besides the stunning view from its observation deck, there's an art exhibit on the 80th floor to explore. And for a truly immersive experience, don't miss the Skyride, a 30-minute virtual tour showcasing the best of what New York City has to offer.

Cost: $29 - $49/person

13 The famous Empire State Building

Empire State Building

Address: 350 5th Ave, New York, NY 10118 Opening Times: Daily from 8 AM to 2 AM. Info: 102 floors. Construction began in 1930. Website: http://www.esbnyc.com/

Review: The Empire State Building offers breathtaking views of NYC, particularly during sunrise and sunset. While special tours are available for these times, be aware that weather conditions like fog may affect visibility. The 86th floor can be chilly, so bring a jacket. Dining options are not available at the observatory, and lines for the elevators can be long. The observatory deck on the 86th floor provides a 360-degree view of NYC, along with a multimedia experience in 8 different languages.

Cost: Book online tickets to the Empire State Building here, costing $35 (€29) per person. Upgrade to the NYC It All: 4-in-one Combination ticket for $110 (€90) per person, which includes standard entrance to the Empire State Building Observatory, Metropolitan Museum of Art ticket, 24-hour Hop-on Hop-off ticket for either the uptown or downtown loop, and your choice of a Harbor Lights or Statue of Liberty cruise.

Tips:

- High-power binoculars are available for an additional fee.
- The Empire State Building is open daily from 8 AM to 2 AM, with the last admission at 1:15 AM.
- Peak entrance times are between 11 AM and 2 PM, as well as 1 hour before and after sunset.
- Mobile vouchers are not accepted; bring a printed copy of your voucher if purchasing tickets online.
- All guests must pass through security to access the Observatory.
- An additional observatory is on the 102nd floor; upgrade your ticket at the Observatory ticket office (2nd floor) or at the 86th-floor kiosk.
- Express Pass: Purchase on-site at the ticket office on the day of arrival to skip lines.
- VIP Express Experience (May to September and December): During peak seasons and public holidays, choose this option to save time. An attendant will greet you on the second floor, issue an exclusive gold VIP wristband, and help you avoid lines for the ticket office. Show your wristband for priority access to and from the observatory.

13:00 Grays Papaya, Lincoln Center, and The Central Park Zoo

Enjoy a quick bite at the renowned Grays Papaya before strolling around Lincoln Center to appreciate its stunning architecture. After soaking in the city's atmosphere, head to the serene oasis of Central Park. While Lincoln Center is situated on the park's west side, you can find the Central Park Zoo directly across town at 64th Street and 5th Avenue.

14 Gray's Papaya is a lovely spot to grab a quick snack

Gray's Papaya Hot Dog Restaurant Address: 2090 Broadway, New York (multiple locations as it's a chain) Opening Times: Open 24 hours, daily. Menu: http://places.singleplatform.com/grays-papaya/menu Busiest Times: 12 PM to 1 PM and 9 PM to 10 PM Prices: A combo of 2 hot dogs and one drink costs $5.

16 The Central Park Zoo

Central Park Zoo

Address: 64th St and 5th Ave, New York

Opening Times: Daily from 10 AM to 5 PM, and until 5:30 PM on Saturdays and Sundays

Animal Types: Polar Bears, Gorillas, Hattie, Seals, Penguins, Red Pandas

Most Popular Time: 1:00 PM to 3:00 PM

Review: A small yet enjoyable zoo. Be sure to catch the feedings of penguins, lions, and seals. A lovely place to spend an hour, and the admission price is reasonable.

Cost: Zoo admission: $12 - $18/person

15:30 Lunch at Serendipity 3, 225 East 60th street

17 Serendipity 3 Restaurant

One of New York City's most renowned restaurants, Serendipity 3 offers a diverse menu that includes everything from exquisite chocolates to caviar. With options to suit everyone's tastes, it's hard to imagine not finding something to love here.

Serendipity 3

Address: 225 E 60th St, New York, NY 10022 Opening Times: Daily from 11:30 AM to 12 AM, open until 1 AM on Fridays and Saturdays Website: http://www.serendipity3.com/ Cost: $10 - $40/person

Review: The food is average, but the desserts truly shine. Be sure to try the Frozen Hot Chocolate.

17:00 See the city at night

What's the only thing you cannot see from the Empire State Building? The Empire State Building. Luckily, we have a solution to that. Check out fantastic views of the city, from **Top of the Rock**. Viewing the city at night is impressive. The Top of the Rock is in the building of the Rockefeller Center. That was a building created by the famous multi-billionaire Rockefeller when everyone was pessimistic about the future in NYC; there was an economic catastrophe, and the US was recovering from the world war. When the Rockefeller Center was built, it was the most massive private building in the history.

18 Broad Angle View from Top of the Rock

Cost and Tips: $29/person. You can book the Top of the Rock Ticket online here. The ticket is flexible, and you can change your date of a visit even after you have paid for it online. This ticket allows you to skip the Public General Admission Line - you may experience a wait in line at the Will Call/Guest Services window depending on the time of day and the season. The local provider does not issue entrance times in advance. When you go to the box office, they will grant you a timed entrance based on availability. It is suggested that you go early in the morning or a few days in advance to receive your admission time as popular time slots can fill up quickly. Moreover, although the average visit is 60 minutes, you are welcome to stay on the observation deck as long as you wish. The last elevator to the observation deck departs at 23:00.

19:00 Dinner at the first pizzeria in the United States, Lombardi's Pizza, 32 Spring Street

In 1897 an Italian immigrant reinvented a staple food into one of the world's most eaten foods. And in 1905, Lombardi's opened and became the birthplace of New York Style pizza.

Lombardi's Pizzeria
Address: 32 Spring St, New York
Opening Times: Daily from 11:30 AM to 11 PM (until 12 AM on Friday and Saturday)
Menu and Prices: http://places.singleplatform.com/lombardis-4/menu
Cost: $10 - $20/person
Review: Nice pizza for a nice price. There is a cue system, but you might have to wait even up to an hour to get a table for two. This is also cash only. It's a touristy place. You will be served in paper plates – be prepared.

20:30 Take a stroll around Little Italy

22 Feast of San Gennaro, Little Italy

Littered with small shops, bars, cafes, and restaurants, Little Italy used to be one of the most populated Italian communities. Although most of the area has made way for the more mainstream fare, there is still a small stretch of area that will transport you to a small village in Italy in the early 1900's

21:30 Have a little fun at Greenwich Village Country Club, 110 University Place

Don't let the name fool you. Greenwich Village Country Club is nothing of the sort. Take a trip inside to have some drinks, and have some fun bowling, playing mini golf, playing arcade games and many more activities.

23 Greenwich Village Country Club

Cost: $30+/person. Package deals start at $39.95 per person (two hours of unlimited beer and a round of mini golf)

12:00 AM Return to Hotel

Return to hotel. Take a cab from GVCC. It should be about an 8-minute ride.

See ZoomTip 2.1 for Day 2 Directions

Cost: $15 for taxi

2nd Day Map in NYC

Here's an online Google Map featuring all the recommended destinations for your second day in NYC. This map will help you easily navigate to each location while you're in the city. Click on the photo or the link below to

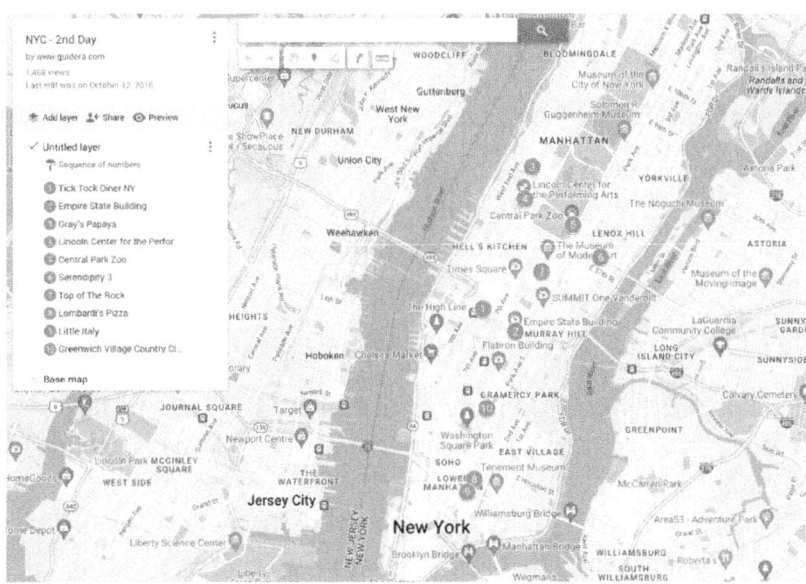

access it.

You can get this map online at
https://drive.google.com/open?id=1kybjw2oL0TAJ5itKgByPgTmEcQk&usp=sharing

Zooming on: Day 2 Directions

Tick Tock Diner (34th Street & 8th Avenue)

Board the uptown #2 train to 34th Street and walk one block west to 8th Avenue. Afterward, stroll east to reach Macy's on 6th Avenue and the Empire State Building on 5th Avenue.

Grays Papaya 2090 Broadway

Head west back towards Macy's. At 7th Avenue, take the uptown #2 train to 72nd Street. Exit at the intersection of West 72nd Street and Amsterdam (Broadway), turn right onto Amsterdam (Broadway), and then turn left onto Broadway. You'll find it on the corner.

Enjoy a leisurely walk downtown towards Lincoln Center.

Turn right onto Columbus Avenue, then left onto Broadway, and finally right onto West 63rd Street. To reach the zoo, either take a taxi or enjoy a walk through the park, which is highly recommended. Enter the park on West 66th Street and continue along 65th Street (Transverse Road). Turn right on 5th Avenue, and you're there. The park walk takes about 15 minutes.

Serendipity 3 225 East 60th Street

Head north on Broadway towards Amsterdam Avenue (Broadway). Turn right onto Amsterdam (Broadway) and then left onto 72nd Street.

Take the M57 bus going towards East Side York. Get off at 57th Street & Lexington. Walk east towards 3rd Avenue, turn left on 3rd Avenue, turn right onto 60th street and you will see the restaurant.

Top of the Rock 45 Rockefeller Plaza

Walk north on Broadway to 72nd Street. Take the downtown #1 train to 59th Street. Transfer to the downtown D train to 47-50 Rockefeller Center. Exit near the intersection of West 50th Street and 6th Avenue. Walk southeast on West 50th Street. Turn left onto Rockefeller Plaza, and you have arrived.

Lombardi's Pizzeria 32 Spring Street

Walk towards Amsterdam Avenue. Turn left onto 72nd street. Take the M5 bus towards South Ferry. Get off at Broadway – Spring Street. Walk northeast on Broadway towards Spring Street. Turn right onto Spring Street... And Little Italy is just up the block on Mott Street.

Greenwich Village Country Club 110 University Place

Walk west on Spring Street towards Mulberry Street. The entrance to the train is on Lafayette and Spring Street. Take the uptown #6 train to 14th street – Union Square. Exit near the intersection of University Avenue and 14th Street. Start walking southwest towards 13th street.

Club Quarters

Take a cab home. It will be about a 10-minute ride and won't cost more than $15.

Day 3: Intrepid Museum, Grand Central

09:00 Breakfast at Amy's Bread, 672 9th Avenue

Enjoy a great Sunday brunch at this neighborhood staple. Great for cupcakes, bread, baguettes, homemade pastries and great coffee. Be sure

to try their Red Velvet cake.

Amy's Bread
Address: 672 9th Ave, New York, NY 10036
Opening Times: Wednesday 7AM–10PM, Thursday 7AM–11PM, Friday 7AM–11PM, Saturday 8AM–11PM, Sunday 8AM–9PM, Monday 7AM–9PM, Tuesday 7AM–10PM
Cost: $5 - $20/person
Menu: http://shop.amysbread.com/collections/bread
Website: http://www.amysbread.com/

10:30 Visit the Intrepid Sea, Air & Space

Come aboard the only museum that lets you step aboard an aircraft carrier to learn about its military history. Also available to see are a submarine, a Concorde airplane, and the all-new Space Shuttle Pavilion.

24 British Airways Concorde G-BOAD as seen from the flight deck of the Intrepid

25 Submarine at the Intrepid Museum

Intrepid Museum
Address: Pier 86, W 46th St & 12th Ave, New York, NY 10036
Time You Need: Usually 2 hours
Opening Times: Daily from 10 AM until 5 PM (and until 6 PM on Saturday and Sunday)
Website: http://www.intrepidmuseum.org/
General Admission: $22/person

Tips: You may need to wait in the lines to visit some exhibits (e.g., the submarine), and if it's a hot day, it will be a little bit uncomfortable. Get some bottles of water with you.

12:00 City Cruise Experience

Join a Circle Line cruise just a short walk from the Intrepid Museum, and embark on a scenic water tour around the entire island of Manhattan. Catch glimpses of the places you didn't have time to visit during your stay,

and bid farewell to this amazing city until your next visit.

Circle Line Cruises
Address: Pier 83, W 42nd St, New York, NY 10036
Opening Times: Daily from 9 AM to 7 PM
Cost: $42/person for the 2.5-hour tour to circle Manhattan. There are some cheaper options too.
Most Popular Times: from 9 AM to 2 PM
Tips: Food and drinks sold on the boat are expensive (e.g., a drink costs 10 USD, and you get in a plastic cup). Do an early check-in to get a comfortable seat. If you want to avoid this cruise, you can get a free ferry to Staten Island. If you book online, you will be asked to arrive 45 minutes before your timeslot, and the boarding starts 30 minutes before the departure time. Be aware that sometimes you may be even an hour before and find huge lines waiting there already. It is a big crowded boat so be patient if you choose this way to cruise around Manhattan. Don't go for their VIP pass, (it costs 100 USD per person but will not make a significant difference to your experience).

You can also use the New York Water Taxi Champaign Cruise which costs **32 USD** or 28 EUR per person. You can book it here. It has a duration of one hour, live commentary in English and you will get a glass of champaign (though in a plastic cup). No luxuries – this is a basic but cheaper way to do an NYC cruise.

26 On board the NYC Water Taxi

27 The NYC Water Taxi boat

The Splurge Option Cruise: NYC Lights Dinner Cruise

Of course, in NYC you can spend as much money as you want for each activity. There is all kind of options from VIP to more economical ways to enjoy everything. And the cruise experience is not an exception to this rule. So, if you are into the splurge option of experiencing a cruise in NYC, you can go for the NYC Lights Dinner Cruise. It costs 180 USD (149 EUR) per person, and you can book it here. It is a three-hour yacht cruise from NYC harbor, with a dinner of 4-course gourmet dishes and a full bar option available for purchase.

28 The NYC Lights Dinner Cruise is the Splurge Option to Experience a Cruise in NYC

15:00 Have a late lunch at Shake Shack, 691 8th Avenue

Grab a quick bite to eat at one of the city's most popular new restaurants

just a few blocks from Times Square.

See ZoomTip 3.1 for Day 3 directions

Shake Shack
Address: 691 8th Ave, New York, NY 10036,
Opening Times: Daily from 11 AM to 12 AM
$10 - $30/person
Menu: http://places.singleplatform.com/shake-shack-2/menu
Website: https://www.shakeshack.com/location/theater-district/
Tips: This is very crowded. People are standing until someone finishes his burger, so expect to eat with some "pressure" above your head. It has beautiful big windows and tasty burgers, fried potatoes and Portobello mushrooms.

16:00 Head back to the hotel to check out
Be sure to arrive at the airport with plenty of time to get through security

18:00 Shopping in the Woodbury Commons Outlet Mall

(to get there book your bus tickets here)

30 The Woodbury Outlet Mall is one hour driving time North of NYC

29 The Woodbury Commons Outlet Mall

This outlet mall features deals from over 200 designer outlets, offering discounts up to 65%. It's open daily, year-round, from 9 AM to 9 PM. Renowned brands such as Balenciaga, Burberry, Chanel, Coach, Chloe, Dolce & Gabbana, Etro, Fendi, Gap Outlet, Giorgio Armani, Gucci, J.Crew/Crewcuts, Jimmy Choo, Lacoste, Neiman Marcus Last Call, Polo Ralph Lauren, Prada, Saks Fifth Avenue Off 5th, Tod's, Tory Burch, and Zegna can be found here.

You'll also receive a complimentary VIP Coupon Book valued at $10, which provides hundreds of dollars in additional savings.

Round-trip transportation from New York City to Woodbury Commons is $45 (€38) per person, as the mall is an hour away from NYC. You can book your bus tickets here.

Review: Woodbury Commons offers many great deals, especially on previous-season items from well-known brands. However, not all brands have extraordinary deals; sometimes, you might find similar items at comparable prices at Macy's in NYC. Overall, if you have the time and desire for an outlet mall experience, it's worth a visit. For those visiting from Europe, it's worth focusing on purchasing deals from US brands (e.g., CK, Hilfiger, DKNY), as European brands (e.g., Diesel) may not be significantly cheaper.

Day 3 NYC Map

Here's an online Google Map featuring all the recommended destinations for your third day in New York City. This map will make it easy for you to quickly navigate to each location while you're in the city. To access the map, simply click on the photo or the link provided below.

31 The Online Google Map with All the Spots of Your Third Day in NYC

Get this map online at
https://drive.google.com/open?id=1jKggaUqp3NBJNBITN6A9HSlZPJU&usp=sharing

Zooming on: Day 3 Directions

Amy's Bread 672 9th Avenue

Take the uptown #2 train to 42nd Street. Exit near the intersection of 44th and 8th Avenue. Walk west on 44th Street. Turn right onto 9th Avenue

Intrepid Sea, Air & Space Museum Pier 83 @ 46th Street and 12th Avenue

Walk west towards 12th Avenue. Turn left on 12th Avenue. It is a huge ship that you can not possibly miss. Just a few blocks down on 42nd street and 12th Avenue is the Circle Line cruise.

Shake Shack 691 8th Avenue

After your cruise, take a walk straight down 42nd. Turn left on 8th Avenue. Shake Shack is one block up.

Club Quarters Take a cab home. Your trip is almost done.

LaGuardia Airport

Take the uptown #2 train to 125th street. Get off and take the M60 bus headed towards LaGuardia Airport. Let the driver know what airline you are flying, and he will let you know your stop.

The Craziest Experience You Can Have in NYC

32 A Helicopter Tour of NYC

This experience may not be for everyone, but we wanted to share it as it could be perfect for those on a special occasion in NYC, such as a honeymoon or a marriage proposal. It's also great for those who simply adore surprises.

The craziest thing you can do in NYC is a helicopter tour of the New York City. It starts at 260 USD (209 EUR) per person, and the duration is from 15 minutes to 30 minutes. As you can imagine this is a one-of-a-kind experience, however not everyone can afford it. You can book it here

On your flight, you will see the beautiful Central Park, Hudson River, and New York Harbor, including the Intrepid Sea Air Space Museum.

You also cruise past the Rockefeller Center, Empire State Building, the World Financial Center, and the Chrysler Building, as well as the iconic Statue of Liberty, Ellis Island, Greenwich Village, South Street Seaport, and the 126-year-old Brooklyn Bridge.

Day Trips from New York City

New York is one of the best destinations in the United States, especially for people who love big, busy cities. A vacation in the Big Apple can be exciting and fun with many things to see and an impressive number of exciting activities. However, it can also be overwhelming for many travelers, and some feel the need to take a break from its busy streets, from the constant honks of taxi cabs and the over packed subways.

When you feel the need to take a breath of fresh air during your vacation in New York, you can always run away from the busy city and spend a few hours or even a day exploring its surroundings. There are many day trips from NYC that you can enjoy with your traveling partners. You only have to choose the one that suits you and prepare yourself for a new adventure. Here are some of the places you can go to when NYC overwhelms you.

Washington D.C. Day Trip from New York City (around 140 USD per person)

Washington D.C is the political capital of the United States, and probably of the world, and you can get to know it on a day trip from NYC. A couple of things you could find the time to see in your day there is the White House, the Mall, the Arlington National Cemetery and you will also see the gravesite of John F. Kennedy. You can book this day trip to Washington DC from NYC here.

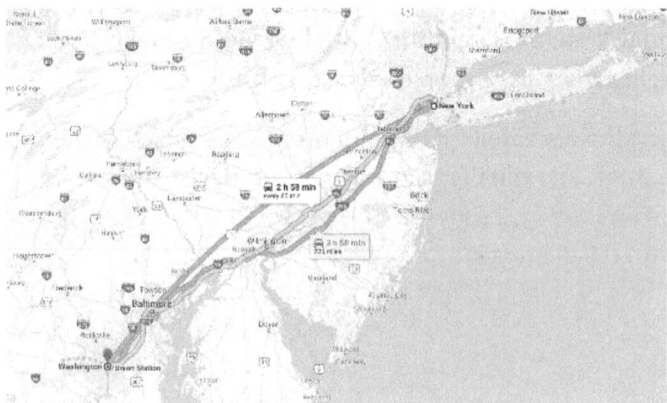

The buses for the day trips to Washington, leave on 07:00 AM from NYC, so you should get prepared for an early start in your day. The distance from NYC to Washington DC is 226 miles, so it is around four hours with the bus. If you don't want to get an organized day tour, you can get the train, which takes 2hours and 53 minutes from NYC to Washington.

Explore the Rich Historical Heritage of Philadelphia

Not many foreigners know that Philadelphia is one of the most visited cities in the United States. However, history enthusiasts recognize the importance of the town and why they should explore it when they have the opportunity. Philadelphia used to be the country's capital before Washington, D.C. became the most important city in the US. Also, both the United States Constitution and the Declaration of Independence were signed in Philly, in Independence Hall

However, there is much more about this city than its history. Besides offering visitors amazing museums, Philly is filled with great restaurants bars, and it has an explosive nightlife.

You can quickly get to Philadelphia by train in just an hour so if you have enough time don't hesitate and visit this fantastic city.

Enjoy a Day in the Middle of Nature at Bear Mountain State Park

NYC is lovely, but many people feel the need to get in touch with nature after a few days in the big city. Sure, you have Central Park, but for some, this is not enough. If you are one of them, grab your hiking boots and go to the Bear Mountain State Park, where you can explore Bear Mountain, West Mountain, and Dunderberg Mountain. Also, you have the chance to enjoy a relaxing bird watching session at the Iona Island Bird Sanctuary in the Hudson River. And if you visit NYC during winter when hiking, swimming and boating are impossible, you can always adventure yourself into sledding or skating.

Also, the park has great activities that can make families who travel with kids extremely happy. While you enjoy a breath of fresh air, your kids can have some fun at the Trailside Museums and Zoo as well as experience the favorite Merry-Go-Round available in the park.

The Bear Mountain State Park is located only an hour and a half far from New York City, and you can quickly get there by car.

Have Some Fun at the Six Flags Great Adventure in New Jersey

If you love theme parks or you travel with your children going to Six Flags in New Jersey can definitely make a great day trip from NYC. The park is a great way to get away from the busy city and spend a day filled with laughter and…screaming, especially if you are planning to adventure yourselves into riding Kingda Ka, the world's tallest and second fastest roller coaster. If you are not that adventurous, don't worry because there are many other amazing things to do in the park. It is definitely a fantastic option for thrill seekers who want to take a break from the charming, but sometimes overwhelming New York City,

The park is located only 90 minutes far from the Big Apple, and you can quickly get there by bus or, if you feel more comfortable, you can rent a car. However, if you travel on a strict budget, the first option is definitely better.

Unwind on a Charming Beach: Fire Island

If you plan to visit NYC during the summer months and you feel the need to get away from the hectic city for a couple of hours, opt for a day trip to Fire Island. Located away from the Atlantic coast of Long Island, this is definitely the piece of heaven you need to go to when New York becomes too much for your peaceful soul.

Grab your flip-flops and prepare yourself to relax while exploring the vast beaches and the beautiful sandy dunes of Fire Island. After this charming experience, you are ready to continue visiting the amazing landmarks of the City that Never Sleeps.

Fire Island is located only 40 minutes far from NYC, and you can get there on a ferry, or you can drive to Robert Moses State Park, and walk or ride a bicycle until you get to your destination.

These are just some of the best day trips from NYC that can be enjoyed during your vacation in the big city, but there are more other exciting spots you can go to whenever the hectic city becomes too much.

Thank You

We hope this comprehensive travel guide has provided you with valuable insights and recommendations for your unforgettable New York City adventure. From iconic landmarks and world-renowned museums to diverse culinary experiences and bustling shopping districts, the city that never sleeps has something for everyone.

As you explore the vibrant streets and immerse yourself in the unique atmosphere of the Big Apple, remember to soak in the moments and create lasting memories. Whether you're a first-time visitor or a seasoned traveler, there's always something new and exciting to discover in New York City.

Safe travels, and enjoy your journey through the captivating and unforgettable metropolis that is New York City!

Your friends at Guidora.

Copyright Notice

Guidora New York City in 3 Days Travel Guide ©

All rights reserved. No part of either publication may be reproduced in any material form, including electronic means, without the prior written permission of the copyright owner.

Text and all materials are protected by UK and international copyright and/or trademark law and may not be reproduced in any form except for non-commercial private viewing or with prior written consent from the publisher, with the exception that permission is hereby granted for the use of this material in the form of brief passages in reviews when the source of the quotations is acknowledged.

Disclaimer

The publishers have checked the information in this travel guide, but its accuracy is not warranted or guaranteed. New York City visitors are advised that opening times should always be checked before making a journey.

Tracing Copyright Owners

Every effort has been made to trace the copyright holders of referred material. Where these efforts have not been successful, copyright owners are invited to contact the editor (Guidora) so that their copyright can be acknowledged and/or the material removed from the publication.

Creative Commons Content

We are most grateful to publishers of Creative Commons material, including images. Our policies concerning this material are (1) to credit the copyright owner, and provide a link where possible (2) to remove Creative Commons material, at once, if the copyright owner so requests - for example, if the owner changes the licensing of an image.

We will also keep our interpretation of the Creative Commons Non-Commercial license under review. Along with, we believe, most web publishers, our current view is that acceptance of the 'Non-Commercial' condition means (1) we must not sell the image or any publication containing the image (2) we may, however, use an image as an illustration for some information which is not being sold or offered for sale.

Note to other copyright owners

We are grateful to those copyright owners who have given permission for their material to be used. Some of the material in the comes from secondary and tertiary sources. In every case we have tried to locate the original author or photographer and make the appropriate acknowledgement. In some cases the sources have proved obscure and we have been unable to track them down. In these cases, we would like to hear from the copyright owners and will be pleased to acknowledge them in future editions or remove the material.

Printed in Great Britain
by Amazon